More WISCONSIN CRimeS OF THE CENTURY

MARV BALOUSEK

w p

Waubesa Press
P.O. Box 192
Oregon, WI 53575

© Copyright 1993 by Marv Balousek

Published by Waubesa Press, Oregon, WI
Edited by Barbara Snell

Cover gun photo by Carolyn Pflasterer

ISBN 1-878569-11-2

Printed by BookCrafters Inc. of Chelsea, MI

All photos used by permission of the Madison Newspapers Inc. newsroom library unless otherwise noted.

*F*or *Barbara*

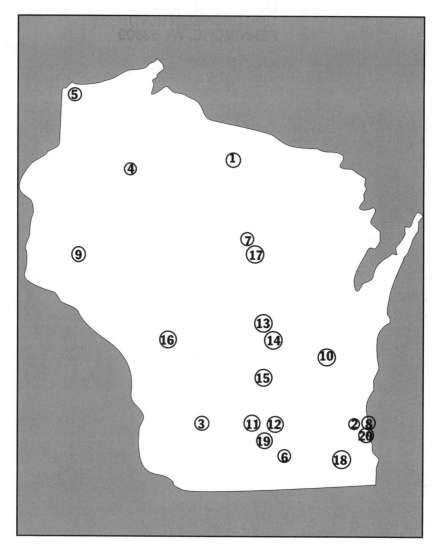

Crimes of the Century locations

Map numbers are placed at the location of the crime
and refer to the chapter number.

Contents

Introduction

When *Wisconsin Crimes of the Century* was published in 1989, the renewed public interest in crime stories was relatively new. Programs depicting criminal cases were just beginning to appear on television. One reason for their popularity is that they are cheap to produce. Another is that the usual spate of television drama can't match the intensity and authenticity of real-life stories.

Today, a half dozen or more true-crime shows appear regularly. They range from a camera that follows regular cops around to portrayals of sensational FBI cases. Several shows use re-enactments of crimes to capture criminals on the run. It's not a new concept. Long before television, bigamist and murderer Jiggs Perry was apprehended when a pair of San Francisco detectives recognized his photo in True Detective Magazine.

Book publishers also have taken note of the renewed public interest in crime. Three books, *The Tangled Web* by John M. Potter, *Crime of Magnitude* by Mark Lemberger and *Rads* by Tom Bates, focus on cases I wrote about in *Wisconsin Crimes of the Century* and all have been published since 1989.

There is no magic formula for selecting cases that qualify as crimes of the century. In this volume, I have selected 20 more Wisconsin criminal cases. As in the first volume, all of these cases stirred considerable public outrage or provided an unusual twist of some kind.

I have included a few unsolved cases in this book, hoping that perhaps someone may yet come forward. These include the kidnapping and murder of Superior newsboy Michael Fisher in 1966 and the slayings of seven women in the Madison area between 1969 and 1982. The Kunz family murders near Wausau in 1987 also remain unsolved, although prime suspect Chris Jacobs was arrested again as this book went to press.

In researching these cases, I am struck by the notion that certain types of crime don't change. The love triangle that involved Waukesha teacher Grace Lusk in 1917, for example, is remarkably similar to the more recent case of Marathon County dairy princess Lori Esker. Mass killers also have always been with us as the 1914 murders at Frank Lloyd Wright's Taliesin estate demonstrate.

Some types of crimes do change, of course, and one is the old-fashioned bank robbery. These days, most bank robberies are committed by perpetrators with drug or mental problems. The 1930s was the heyday of the robber gang such as the most famous one led by John Dillinger. Another Dillinger contemporary was Francis Keating, who led a Twin Cities gang and committed a murderous 1931 robbery at the Kraft State Bank in Menomonie. Dillinger captured the public's fancy with his Robin Hood antics but the brutal Keating and his cohorts had no such redeeming charm.

I have included two recent well-publicized cases because there is no question that they are two of Wisconsin's most notorious crimes. One is the case of Jeffrey Dahmer, who murdered and dissected 17 men and boys in Milwaukee before his capture in 1991. I co-authored a book on the Dahmer case, *Massacre in Milwaukee*, with my Wisconsin State Journal colleague Richard Jaeger.

The other case, the murder of Christine Schultz by Lawrencia "Bambi" Bembenek, also has received considerable publicity. However, I believe the version of this crime that has spawned books and television movies isn't necessarily the accurate one. It makes a better television movie to portray Bembenek as a woman victimized by the judicial system but evidence remains that she was no innocent deer caught in the headlight glare of the criminal justice system as her nickname would imply. She was a streetwise cop who, since her release, has alienated some of those who helped win her freedom. Read Chapter 2 for a different version of this case.

Other cases have been left out that certainly would be listed among Wisconsin's worst crimes. An example is the recent conviction of Bruce Benizer for the brutal murders of several family members. Another is the Barbara Hoffman case, detailed in an excellent book, *Winter of Frozen Dreams* by Karl Harter. As I have indicated, the cases included in this book are not a definitive list of the state's worst. Besides selecting what I believe are interesting stories, I also tried to achieve some semblance of geographical and chronological balance.

I must make one correction regarding the first book. The only major error of which I'm aware was that the name of Theodore Brazeau was misspelled. Brazeau was a talented attorney known as "The Little Giant of Wisconsin Rapids" who prosecuted mailbox bomber John Magnuson. My apologies to the Brazeau family. I'm not sure whether the misspelling was the result of a source's error or my own selective dyslexia that caused me to transpose the letters.

Besides Richard Jaeger, mentioned previously, I also want to thank another State Journal colleague, George Hesselberg, a popular columnist and former police reporter who was very helpful in unearthing possible cases to include in this book. Thanks also to Ron Larson, the librarian at Madison Newspapers Inc., who helped collect photos for this book and the previous one. Jerry Carlson, Hancock village clerk and local historian, also deserves my gratitude for the information he provided about the Elmer Huckins fraud case.

Once again, I also pay tribute to the crime reporters throughout the state who provided much of the detail about these cases in their dispatches often written under the pressures of daily deadlines.

In the introduction to *Wisconsin Crimes of the Century*, I wrote about the need to understand these cases in hopes of preventing similar crimes in the future. This, of course, is not an easy task but it is an important challenge for all of us. Aiming the spotlight of publicity at unsolved crimes has proven successful in caputuring fugitives but we need to go beyond that. We must study these crimes with a thought of trying to discovering what is wrong with our society that allows them to occur.

A proposed handgun ban was defeated in Madison in early 1993 by a narrow margin. The proposal generated the usual pros and cons. Whether or not that proposal was a good idea, at least it was a concrete plan for coping with the escalating problems of guns and drugs in that city.

European cities don't have the kind of problems we do with crime and violence. In Toronto, the robbery of a convenience store, a rather unusual event in that city, prompts extensive media coverage. In our country, scores of murders in big cities don't merit a mention in daily newspapers unless they have some kind of twist or involve someone prominent.

What causes our high rate of crime and violence? Is it greed built into our system? Is it a deep-seated societal disregard for the value of human life? Is it rooted in conflicting struggles among races or economic classes?

These are questions worth pondering.

— Marv Balousek
July 1993

Chapter 1

The Keys to Her Heart
Lac du Flambeau, 1930

San Francisco Police Detective James Johnson was thumbing through the July 1931 issue of True Detective magazine when he came across a story about George "Jiggs" Perry written by Rhinelander Daily News reporter Jack Cory. Perry, it seemed, was wanted for murdering one of several women he married. Johnson read part of the story but stopped when he spotted a picture of Perry. He motioned for inspectors Robert Hughes and A.P. James to come over and take a look.

"That's the same man we questioned two months ago in connection with an automobile accident," he said, pointing at the picture. "I'm sure of it."

The detectives checked an address and then rushed out to arrest a man they believed could be a Wisconsin killer. But they didn't find Perry. Instead, they arrested Frank Moran, who claimed he knew nothing about the Wisconsin slaying.

During the year he was on the run, Perry had gained notoriety as "the marrying brakeman." A former railroad employee, he had married and deserted more than a half dozen women from Cleveland to California.

George "Jiggs" Perry

On Sept. 30, 1930, Henry St. Germaine, a watchtower attendant at the Lac du Flambeau Indian reservation, was walking in the woods when his dog led him to what looked at first like a pile of rumpled clothing.

"I didn't want to believe it was a body," he said later. "It looked more like a scarecrow."

But it was a body — the body of Cora Belle Hackett, in fact — one of the many wives of Jiggs Perry. A warrant was issued a week later for Perry's arrest. He was tracked to Cleveland, where another wife was discovered. The trail then led to southern Illinois, where still another wife turned up. Authorities lost Perry's trail, however, in Blytheville, Ark., where they found yet another woman he had married.

Cora Belle had disappeared July 6, 1930, while she and Perry, her new husband, were honeymooning at the Crawling Lake Resort, owned by William Parker in Vilas County. Perry borrowed a rifle from Parker, then the couple left for awhile. Perry returned without his bride, paid the bill and left with her luggage in her car.

Katherine Gebhardt, his wife in Cleveland, got a call from him the next day asking if he could come home. He was in Racine and had car trouble. He told her that his Aunt Cora had given him some belongings and her car. Gebhardt reluctantly agreed that Perry could return home but she didn't get along very well with him. By the end of July, Perry left Cleveland and was on the run again.

Cora Belle, who worked selling lifetime memberships to Chicago's Art Institute, had been widowed twice. She had been married to a Milwaukee banker and, later, to a U.S. Secret Service agent. She met Perry by answering his blind ad in a Chicago newspaper for a traveling companion. Perry told her he was the outcast son of a wealthy family and asked her to marry him. She agreed to finance their honeymoon.

When the inspectors in San Francisco came to arrest Moran that day in July 1931, they weren't willing to take Moran's word for it that he wasn't the fugitive Perry. They contacted the Vilas County sheriff at Eagle River to tell him of the capture. The sheriff began the process of trying to determine whether Moran actually was the missing killer.

After viewing a photo of Moran, the sheriff was convinced the man in custody probably was Perry. He sent a warrant by air mail to San Francisco, then arranged a train trip to the West Coast. Accompanying him to aid in positive identification was resort owner Parker, who knew Perry well.

When he was taken into custody, Moran was employed as business manager for the International Brotherhood, a welfare agency. He had married Anna Guiterrez after a whirlwind courtship.

The sheriff and Parker visited Moran's cell and he still denied that he was Perry. Parker noticed, however, that Moran kept referring to his California jailers as "them guys," a Wisconsin expression. When Parker pointed it out, Perry admitted his true identity.

"I did not kill Cora Hackett," he said. "It's bad enough to be guilty of bigamy, non-support and many other crimes without being guilty of murder."

Reporters contacted Perry's only legal wife, Mary Perry of Milwaukee, and she could not believe her husband was guilty.

Several reporters were among the entourage escorting Perry by train back to Wisconsin and he was willing to give interviews, although for awhile he insisted the reporters call him Moran.

"Oh, what's the use," he said finally. "I'm Perry and you know it. There's nothing I can do but take the raps. I'm guilty of bigamy, plenty guilty, but not of murder."

In fact, Perry had married seven women illegally within a little more than a year. On Jan. 3, 1930, he married Katherine Gebhardt in a secret ceremony in Chicago. Using the same ruse, he would later use to lure Cora Belle Hackett, Perry told her he was heir to a fortune. For several months, she supported him with income from her seamstress job while he lounged around their Cleveland home and read the newspaper. In early June, he left for Chicago, saying he had some family business to settle.

On June 16, Perry married Cora Belle Hackett. In several letters to Gebhardt, he talked about his Aunt Cora and said he would be traveling with her to northern Wisconsin. In a letter to her best friend in Chicago, Cora Belle said she was extremely happy with her new husband.

When Perry called her on July 7, Gebhardt said he could return home. He arrived "a changed man," she said, with Hackett's clothing, luggage and car. He seemed "extremely irritable."

In late July, Gebhardt received a call from another woman who asked if she was married to Perry. Gebhardt told the other woman Perry was her husband.

"Why he can't be!" the woman said. "He proposed to me and promised me $18,000 after we were married in Chicago."

The phone call led to a bitter argument between Gebhardt and Perry and Perry departed. He landed in Eldorado, Ill., where he married Lida Downey. That ceremony was quickly followed by another marriage to Elizabeth Manson of Harrisburg, Ill. Perry began to worry that he had two wives living too close together so he was on the run again.

In Blytheville, Ark., Perry put Hackett's car in storage as collateral for a $150 loan and married Dorothy Davis before moving on to St. Louis, where he married Harriet Milligan after one of his trademarked whirlwind courtships. Perry still used his own name but claimed he was from New Orleans. Milligan noticed Perry's name mentioned in a newspaper article about the Hackett case. She pointed it out to him and he was on the run once again, this time to San Francisco.

In Milwaukee, the original Mrs. Perry hoped the sheriff would bring her husband by to see her and their three children on the way back to Eagle River.

"I would like to see him," she said. "Only then would I believe it is really Jiggs. I have been awake for every hour of the night for the past two weeks, worrying."

But the entourage bypassed Milwaukee and Perry was placed in the Vilas County Jail. On June 5, he pleaded not guilty to first degree murder.

The master philanderer turned to his stable of wives for help, asking each of them to come up with his bail. "Write me, and if you can, help me," he wrote to Anna Guiterrez. None of the wives responded. In Cleveland, Katherine Gebhardt filed for divorce.

Perry appealed to Milwaukee attorney John Dolan to represent him. Dolan and Perry once worked together at a moving and storage company.

"Am not guilty of this crime I am accused of and, with the help of a good attorney, can be freed," he wrote. Dolan agreed to take the case.

"Perry may be the world's greatest lover but he certainly is no killer," Dolan announced after meeting with his new client. Accompanying him to Eagle River were Mary Perry and her children.

"Mary, Mary, Mary," Perry greeted his original wife, who carried their 21-month-old daughter, Grace, in her arms. "Hello, dad," said son Danny while their other son, Johnny, bragged to his father about fistfights he had with reporters and photographers who lurked outside the family's Milwaukee home.

"Why did you marry all those women?" Mary wanted to know. Perry just hung his head. "Well," he said, followed by a long silence. Finally, she decided to change the subject. "I brought you some oranges, George."

With his head held high and shoulders back, Perry strutted into the courtroom when the trial began on July 30. He had an ironclad alibi, he had bragged to reporters. But Perry soon became shaken when Dr. E.W. Miloslavich, a Milwaukee pathologist, held up Cora Belle's skull, describing how she had been shot once through the left side of her head. Perry's face twitched and he clenched his fists. The ironclad alibi fell apart when witnesses from Minocqua refused to testify on his behalf.

The most damaging testimony was provided by Mrs. Michael Dever, wife of a Chicago police officer, who said she recognized Perry as the man she saw on July 6, 1931, standing next to a car parked along the roadside near where the body was found. Katherine Gebhardt also testified for the prosecution and Perry shifted nervously when she described his claims of great wealth.

Perry took the stand in his own defense and the courtroom went into an uproar with the first question by Dolan.

"Are you married?" the attorney asked.

"Yes," Perry replied.

Perry claimed he had told Cora Belle the truth, that they

weren't really married, and she was disappointed, not angry. She said they couldn't live together anymore. But she generously agreed to give him her car and some of her clothing for his real wife. They parted on the roadside at the Indian reservation and someone else must have killed her, according to the story.

"I didn't know Cora Belle was dead," Perry said, feigning great sincerity. "I cried and paced the floor because I was married to Katherine. I was sorry for that mix-up and wanted to get home."

During his testimony, of course, Perry must have lost track of his wives, forgetting that he actually was married only to Mary, who maintained a vigil with the children in the courtroom to show support for him. The all-male jury didn't buy Perry's flimsy tale. He collapsed in his chair when the jury returned a guilty verdict, then went on a petulant hunger strike in jail.

He was sentenced to life in prison and carted off to Waupun State Prison, handcuffed to insane killer Phil Block and John Adams, a convicted burglar.

"I'm sure Mr. Perry is innocent," said the faithful Mary after the trial. "Someone else killed her, not Mr. Perry."

Mary Perry said she would have to remain on welfare because the children were too young to work and she couldn't leave them alone.

The Jiggs Perry case is remarkably similar to that of William Coffey, another bigamist-murderer convicted in 1927 of killing Hattie Sherman Hales on their honeymoon and burying her remains in Bratton's Woods near Platteville. Unlike Perry, Coffey had only two wives. After killing Hattie, he continued their honeymoon without her, writing regular letters to Hattie's sister and forging his dead wife's name with a rubber stamp. But the sister became suspicious, which led to Coffey's capture. The Coffey case is featured in the first volume of *Wisconsin Crimes of the Century*.

Like Coffey, Perry bragged of his power over women to get them to do his bidding. He once invited his nephew to join him in the love scam business.

"It's all a game," he said. "Easy money. Women fall for the love stuff and then you can get their money. Give me two weeks with any woman and she will give me the keys to her heart."

Chapter 2

Bambi's flight to freedom
Milwaukee, 1981

As Sean Schultz awoke, he felt something tighten around his neck, perhaps some kind of rope or wire. He opened his eyes just in time to see a large gloved hand slam down across his nose and mouth. Young Sean screamed, awakening his younger brother, and both boys began to struggle with the assailant. Shannon would say later that the assailant had a reddish ponytail and wore a fatigue jacket.

Suddenly, the figure bounded from the room and across the hall to their mother's bedroom. The boys were still shaking as they heard their mother's voice: "Please don't do that!" They heard a noise that sounded like a firecracker and the boys ran to the other bedroom. They caught a glimpse of the dark figure hunched over their mother's bed before the assailant fled from the room and down the stairs.

Christine Schultz, the boys' mother, had been fatally shot in the back. A scarf also was wrapped around her neck. Her death about 2 a.m. on May 28, 1981, touched off one of Wisconsin's most fascinating murder mysteries — the case of Lawrencia "Bambi" Bembenek.

Elfred Schultz, Christine's ex-husband, was on duty as a Milwaukee police officer at the time his wife was shot. When he received

word of the shooting, Schultz rushed home to comfort his two terrified sons, then joined in the investigation. His colleagues quickly ruled
him out as a suspect. After all, he was on duty when the mysterious
assailant broke into his ex-wife's home.

Based on the description given by Sean and Shannon, police
began a manhunt for an assailant with a red ponytail who wore a green
Army fatigue jacket. A neighbor told detectives someone had broken into his garage on the night of the murder and stolen a green
jogging suit and a .38-caliber revolver.

At the time of the murder, Lawrencia Bembenek, the current
wife of Elfred Schultz, said she was home alone, sleeping. She was
awakened shortly before 3 a.m. by a call from her husband, who said
he had just found out that Christine was murdered. About 4 a.m.,
two detectives rang her doorbell. They asked if she owned a gun or a
green jogging suit. She said no and they left.

An hour later, Elfred arrived with his partner, Micahel Durfee.
Durfee checked Schultz' off-duty revolver and found that it hadn't
been fired. Later, a spot of blood was found on Schultz' regular service revolver. He took a polygraph test and passed, but Bembenek
refused to take the test. Her husband told investigators he had seen
her playing with the bullets in his service revolver a few days before
the murder.

Within three weeks, the focus of the case shifted to Lawrencia
Bembenek. A woman named Judy Zess, a former roommate of
Bembenek's, came forward and told investigators she had heard
Bembenek threaten to kill Christine Schultz. Bembenek was angry,
according to Zess, that the murder victim demanded so much ali-
mony from Elfred Schultz. Bembenek also was jealous of her
husband's first wife, police were told, and wondered whether Elfred
still spent time with her.

The case seemed circumstantial until a reddish brown wig was
discovered in the plumbing of the building where Bembenek and
Elfred Schultz shared an apartment. On June 24, Lawrencia
Bembenek was arrested for the murder of Christine Schultz. Her at-
tractiveness made that case an instant worldwide sensation. She had
worked as a model and as a waitress at the Playboy Club in Lake

Geneva. She also was a former Milwaukee police officer.

Investigators decided Bembenek probably put on a green jogging suit and grabbed her husband's off-duty revolver. Then, she jogged to Christine Schultz' home about two miles away. After trying to strangle Sean and killing his mother, she jogged back home.

The case was solved, or so it appeared. Bembenek spent three days in a holding cell. She was represented at her initial appearance by Richard Reilly, her husband's divorce attorney. But she soon hired Donald Eisenberg, a flashy Madison attorney who enjoyed notoreity and high-profile cases. He promised Bembenek the case would be dismissed at the preliminary hearing. He requested a $25,000 retainer to take the case.

But the charges against Bembenek would not go away that easily. Two startling bits of testimony ensured that she would stand trial for murder. Judy Zess, her neighbor across the hall, told the court that Bembenek once told her she would pay to have Christine Schultz "blown away." And Bembenek's husband was granted immunity from prosecution in exchange for his testimony against her.

At the time of her arrest, Bembenek was working as a Marquette University security guard. Before that, however, she had worked for the Milwaukee police department. At the time, the chief was Harold Brier who didn't have a reputation as a progressive law enforcement leader. In fact, Brier's department came under fire from the black community when Ernest Lacy, a black man, died while in police custody on July 9, 1981. Police had taken him into custody for a rape it later was determined he didn't commit.

Under Brier, the department was equally insensitive about women officers as it was about black suspects. During one week in August 1980, Brier fired three women officers. Among them was Lawrencia Bembenek. When Bembenek finally was allowed to read her file, she discovered the reason for her dismissal was that Judy Zess had signed a statement accusing her of smoking marijuana at a concert.

Out of work, Bembenek landed a job as a waitress at the Lake Geneva Playboy Club. Despite the testimony of Zess that cost her police job, the two women remained friends. She discovered other

Lawrencia Bembenek in a 1986 photo.

Milwaukee police officers weren't so pristine when she saw nude photos taken of officers at a picnic sponsored by a local tavern. One of the officers posing naked was Fred Schultz.

Bembenek continued to fight to get her police job back, even showing some of the nude photos to one of her old friends on the force. She also began dating Schultz after he broke off a relationship with one of her friends, Marjorie Lipschultz.

Later, as she sat in jail charged with murder, she may have wondered whether the charges against her were in retaliation for her battle against the department. Although the testimony of Fred Schultz wasn't as devastating as the testimony of Judy Zess, she felt betrayed. Fred cried at the preliminary hearing, appearing distraught over his ex-wife's murder. Zess testified that Bembenek once told her it would pay to have Christine Schultz blown away. The testimony was enough to bind Bembenek over for trial, despite the assertion by Sean Schultz that his mother's assailant that night was a man in an Army fatigue jacket, not a woman in a jogging suit.

After the hearing, she was free on bond and tried to patch things up with Fred but too much damage apparently had been done to the relationship. The way Bembenek later told it, the tension between them erupted into a shoving match and Fred kicked her, knocking her to the ground. The police were called and Bembenek went home with her father. The story about Milwaukee's most glamorous murder suspect made the papers the next day.

Bembenek's trial began Feb. 23, 1982. Her attorney, Donald Eisenberg, moved to dismiss the case for lack of evidence — a routine motion that is routinely denied.

In his opening arguments, prosecutor Robert Kramer described how Bembenek had jogged to the Schultz house that night, started to strangle Sean and then went to Christine's bedroom and shot her. Defense attorney Eisenberg said his case would hinge on the testimony of Sean Schultz, whose description of the killer did not match Lawrencia Bembenek. He also asked why it took police 21 days to arrest his client.

During his testimony, young Sean again insisted that his mother's murderer was a man. But Judy Zess again told of

Bembenek's comment of having Christine Schultz killed. This time, she even provided more detail, saying that Bembenek actually asked her once about having a murder contract taking out on Schultz.

Day after day, the media circus trial dragged on. Fred Schultz testified that he accused his wife of playing with his bullet pouch but added he didn't think she had access to his off-duty revolver. Eisenberg scored a point against Schultz' partner, Michael Durfee, who claimed to have destroyed all of his records on the case.

On March 4, Lawrencia Bembenek took the stand. She testified for five hours, providing details about how she met Fred Schultz, the nature of their relationship and her actions on the night of the murder. She also testified about harassment from the Milwaukee Police Department related to the fight to win her job back.

On cross examination, Kramer tried to portray Bembenek as a greedy woman driven to kill so her husband would no longer have to pay child support. But the cross examination wasn't nearly as devastating as two additional witnesses who would follow. Marilyn Gehrt testified that, a year earlier, she sold Bembenek a wig. Annette Wilson, a security guard at the Boston Store, testified that Bembenek once stole a green jogging suit from the store. The damaging testimony of Gehrt and Wilson tied Bembenek directly to the evidence in the circumstantial case.

After weeks of testimony, it wasn't surprising that closing arguments would be lengthy. Kramer repeated his theory that Bembenek killed Schultz so Fred could stop paying child support and they could sell the Ramsey Street house for more money. Eisenberg spent five hours reviewing his case in intricate detail. Jurors also took their time. They asked to visit the apartment complex where Bembenek and Fred Schultz lived. Kramer refused the request. The jury also requested portions of the trial transcript to review. On March 9, after several days of deliberations, the jury found Lawrencia Bembenek guilty of the first-degree murder of Christine Schultz.

The public reaction to the verdict was double-edged. Some people viewed Lawrencia Bembenek as a black widow spider, beautiful but deadly. Others could not believe such an attractive woman would commit such a horrible crime. In February 1983, the Appeals

Court upheld the conviction.

Like many inmates, Bemebenek began immediately to prove her innocence. She was supported by hundreds of letters from sympathizers throughout the nation. Public pressure also was brought on the Milwaukee County District Attorney to reopen the case, especially after Eisenberg was accused of impropriety in the Barbara Hoffman murder case for representing two conflicting clients.

The interest of Milwaukee investigator Ira Robins in the Bembenek case apparently began with a 1984 tip from his mechanic, according to an account in *Run, Bambi, Run* by Oconomowoc teacher and writer Kris Radish. The mechanic said he had heard that a wig was planted as evidence that would tie her to the Schultz killing.

The tip piqued Robins' interest in the case so much that he began a one-man crusade to free Bembenek over the next eight years. He was so tenacious and unflagging that Bembenek referred to him affectionately as "my personal bulldog."

What really motivated Robins isn't clear. Perhaps the 42-year-old investigator developed a secret infatuation for the beautiful convict. Maybe he sought the notoriety of an association with her. He may have identified with her struggle with Milwaukee police since he was an former officer himself who suffered discrimination over his Jewish heritage. It could have been he truly was convinced of her innocence and sought justice. In any case, Robins became Bembenek's man on the outside, using his detective skills to follow up her leads and try to find another suspect.

The motives of Jacob Wissler were easier to figure out. He was infatuated with Bembenek and devised a hit-man theory to get close to her. He offered $20,000 to Joey Hecht, convicted of the 1983 murder of Carolyn Hudson in Madison, if Hecht would confess to killing Christine Schultz. From prison, Hecht had been bragged that the Hudson murder wasn't his only contract killing. (The Carolyn Hudson case is detailed in Chapter 19.) Wissler also offered Michael Durfee (Fred Schultz' partner) a $25,000 bribe to retract his testimony. Meanwhile, Wissler was writing a series of love letters to Bemebenek in prison. By this time, she had hired a new attorney, Thomas Halloran.

Halloran was replaced in 1986 by Martin Kohler. Robins continued to plod along in his effort to find something that would shake the state's case against Bemebenek. He spotted similarities between the Schultz murder and a robbery at Judy Zess' apartment. In prison, Bembenek worked on a bachelor's degree and became interested in inmate rights.

Based on Robins' research and Eisenberg's improprieties, Kohleer filed a motion for a new trial in 1987. After some delays and a hearing, Judge Michael Skwierawski denied the motion in November 1988. Several months later, Kohleer filed an appeal of Skwierawski's ruling. That, too, was denied.

Despite repeated rebuffs in court, public fascination about the Bembenek case continued to build. In 1989, the first of many movies about the case was made by a small-time filmmaker. In the public mind, her character was dramatic and exciting. She was an innocent woman framed for murder and beaten down by the judicial system. Robins and Bembenek's parents formed a support group to raise money for her defense.

Nick Gugliatto was visiting his sister at Taycheedah state prison when Bembenek first saw him. Soon afterward, she began corresponding with him. Their correspondence turned to romance and they planned to marry. On July 15, 1990, less than a month after the Court of Appeals denied Bembenek's request for a new trial, she climbed over the prison fence and fled with Gugliatto to Canada.

The escape reopened the public's fascination with the case. In Milwaukee, Robins tried to capitalize on the renewed interest, organizing a rally and enlisting public support for a new trial. Her picture was splashed across TV screens until, finally in October, a tip to the program "America's Most Wanted" led police to her in Thunder Bay, Ontario, where she was working as a waitress under the name of Jennifer Lee Gazzana.

Bembenek's fight against extradition piqued the interest of Canadian authorities. Her dramatic escape and capture also generated more than a little interest from U.S. authors and moviemakers. In the bright eye of publicity, Bembenek seemed to forget her romantic promises to Gugliatto, who was sentenced to a year in the

Fond du Lac County Jail for his role in the escape. Mary Woeherer had replaced Kohler as Bembenek's latest attorney in Milwaukee. Woeherer filed a motion for a secret John Doe investigation into the case and it was granted by Judge William Haese.

On Nov. 30, 1991, Frederick Horenberger shot and killed himself after commiting an armed robbery. Horenberger had evolved as Robins' prime suspect in the Christine Schultz murder. Just before he died, Horenberger denied killing Schultz. But Robins couldn't give up the notion that easily. He reasoned that Horenberger committed suicide rather than become the target of the John Doe probe.

During Bembenek's stay in Canada, she negotiated a publishing deal to write a book titled *Woman on the Run*. In this country, Son of Sam laws, named after the notorious New York City serial killer, often prohibit convicted criminals from profiting by their crimes. She got around those laws, in part, because the book was published in Canada.

At one time, more than a half dozen authors had books in the works on the Bembenek case. Only two, however, were published. Books that argued in favor of her guilt never saw the light of print. They didn't fit the public's popular conception of the case.

After more than a decade behind bars, Bembenek finally won her freedom in 1992. Ironically, it wasn't because a jury or judge finally decided she was innocent. Instead, she agreed to plead no contest to a reduced charge of second-degree murder.

Three TV movies later, some cracks began to appear in the Bembenek fable. Nick Gugliatto complained that he was abandoned by his lover immediately after their arrest. He said her parents helped in the escape. Ira Robins also had become disenchanted with his heroine. He hoped some of the big movie money might help defray some of his expenses over the years in trying to win Bembenek's freedom. Like Gugliatto, she apparently dropped Robins when he wasn't useful to her anymore.

The movies and books so far on the Bembenek case haven't really cleared up the mystery of who killed Christine Schultz. They have only reinforced the public perception of Bembenek as an unfortunate victim of the judicial system. In *Run, Bambi, Run,* author

Kris Radish speculates that perhaps the women on the jury resented Bembenek's beauty. But her beauty clearly was a double-edged sword. If she were unattractive, it's likely she still would be in prison.

A case still can be made for Bembenek's guilt. The two people who stood to gain the most from the death of Christine Schultz were Bembenek and her husband, Fred. But would Fred try to haphazardly strangle his son? Despite the portrait of him as a moral degenerate painted in books about the case, that's unlikely. The judicial conspiracy against Bembenek also appears unnaturally broad. Did the entire Milwaukee Police Department conspire to frame her for murder because she protested her firing? Were the jury and several judges in on the plot? It seems incredulous.

E. Michael McCann has been Milwaukee County district attorney for 25 years. His office has prosecuted many high-profile cases, from Bembenek to Jeffrey Dahmer. After all the evidence unearthed by Robins, all the appeals and all the TV movies, McCann remains convinced of her guilt. "I believe she committed the homicide and that she's left a tragic wake of sorrow," he told the Milwaukee Journal in May 1993.

The nickname "Bambi" was assigned to Bembenek by the media. It is a nickname she neither sought nor particularly likes. It characterizes her as an innocent victim caught in the headlight glare of the criminal justice system. Charged suddenly with a horrendous crime, she reacted like a deer, too frozen to move while the justice system rumbled over her like a two-ton truck. Whether she is guilty of murder or not, it's clear that Bembenek is no Bambi. When the murder occurred she was a street-wise cop. Now, the alienation of those who helped win her freedom demonstrates a strong dose of self-centeredness. She recently has taken to the lecture circuit, collecting fees for her speeches and promoting her book. But self-centeredness and street wisdom do not necessarily add up to murder.

Did Lawrencia Bembenek, the former Playboy Club waitress and police officer, put on her green jogging suit and kill Christine Schultz that night? It's a mystery that may never be resolved definitively.

Chapter 3

Tragedy at Taliesin
Spring Green, 1914

O n Aug. 15, 1914, newspaper headlines blared about impend-
ing war in Europe. The murder of the Serbian Archduke
Ferdinand had solidified the battle lines and, now, Italy and Japan
were threatening to join the fray.

In Spring Green, Wisconsin, Julian Carlton had troubles of
his own. The night before, he had been fired as a cook at Taliesin,
the hillside home of renowned architect Frank Lloyd Wright. The
reason for Carlton's dismissal wasn't clear but he apparently had been
given notice and he certainly wasn't happy about it. The architect
himself was in Chicago supervising construction of the Midway Gardens. But as Carlton prepared what would be his last lunch for members of the Taliesin household, he mulled over a plan of revenge.

The Taliesin household, including Mamah Borthwick and her
two children plus architects and groundskeepers, gathered in the dining room that day as usual to sample Carlton's meal. This time, however, he had a surprise in store for them. First, he blocked all en-
trances but one. Then he grabbed a container of gasoline and poured
some on Tom Blunkert, 60, as he sat at the table. Carlton may have

been jealous that Blunkert, a laborer, was permitted to dine with Mamah and her guests.

Blunkert jumped up and the other diners were startled but, before they could react, Carlton had poured more gasoline on the carpet and struck a match, igniting Blunket and the carpet in a wall of flames.

As flames and smoke engulfed the dining room, the panicked diners got up to flee. They found the doors blocked and began to flee through an unlocked window.

Outside that window, Carlton awaited with a shingler's hatchet held high. As the diners came out to flee the blaze, he swung the axe, trying to kill them one by one. When the slaughter was finished, Carlton decided to take his own life. He swallowed muriatic acid, burning his throat, then fled to the boiler room, where he hoped to burn up in the fire.

In the fields near the Taliesin estate, farm hands operated their threshing machines. They spotted the blaze and rushed to Wright's home, forming a bucket brigade to douse the fire. Outside the dining room, they discovered eight victims of Carlton's wrath.

Mamah Borthwick, 35, Wright's lover, crawled several feet before she collapsed and died. Borthwick's daughter, Martha Cheney, 9, was rushed to the home of Andrew Porters a half mile away, where she died a few hours later. Emil Brodelle, 26, a draftsman from Chicago, died instantly from Carlton's blows with the hatchet. Also killed were Borthwick's son, John, 12, and Ernest Weston, 15, son of William Weston, 65, a construction foreman at Taliesin.

William Weston suffered hatchet wounds on his head but survived only because he stumbled while coming out the door and caught only a glancing blow from Carlton's weapon. Carlton split open the head of Blunkert, who died a few days later. Herbert Fritz, 23, a draftsman, suffered burns but survived. David Lindbloom, 45, the gardener, was not so lucky. He would die of severe burns several days later, becoming the seventh victim of Carlton's rage.

Within hours of the attack, Wright received a strange telegram in Chicago.

"Come as quickly as you possibly can," the telegram read.

"Something terrible has happened." The telegram was signed by Mamah Borthwick. It remains a mystery to this day whether Mamah had a premonition, sending the telegram before she died, or, more likely, whether someone signed her name to it.

When Wright received word that Mamah had been brutally murdered, he collapsed.

"I can't believe it!" he said upon regaining consciousness. "It's too horrible! She was a good woman, the best on earth. She stood everything so bravely."

Newspaper headlines trumpeted that Borthwick, Wright's adulterous lover, had been murdered at their "love castle" or "love bungalow," as Taliesin had come to be known.

Frank Lloyd Wright

"The insane act of a negro cook today ended the strange romance of Frank Lloyd Wright, Chicago architect of worldwide fame and staunch advocate of free love," said the Wisconsin State Journal in a front-page story.

The romance of Wright and Mamah Borthwick made headlines a few years earlier when the lovers spirited off to Europe, abandoning their respective families. Wright left his wife, Catherine, and six children while Borthwick deserted her husband, Edward Cheney, and two children.

When the couple returned, Wright appeared to patch up the differences with his wife while Mrs. Cheney filed for divorce. Then, Wright and Mrs. Cheney disappeared again. He brought her to Wisconsin and they settled in at Taliesin. He had met Mamah Borthwick Cheney in Oak Park, Ill., when he was commissioned by her hus-

Wright's Taliesin home

band to design a house for them.

Now, his beloved Mamah was dead and Wright rushed to catch the next train to Wisconsin. At the station, he met the spurned husband, Edward Cheney, and the two men rode together.

Meanwhile, the killer Carlton remained in hiding. The muriatic acid burned his throat but didn't cause his death as he had hoped. And the fire, which caused extensive damage, was extinguished. Several hours later, a weary Carlton opened the boiler room door and fell out of his hiding place into the hands of Iowa County deputies. Had he been spotted earlier by neighbors fighting the fire, Carlton almost surely would have been lynched. Instead, he was rushed to the Iowa County Jail, where he was unable to eat for several days due to the burns to his throat.

"It was self-defense," Carlton claimed. "They were all picking on me and I had to fight for my life. I took the acid and tried to burn myself up in the furnace." His wife, who lived with him at Taliesin, fled when her husband began his murder spree and vowed to divorce him afterward. She told officials he had no history of drug use.

Thunder clapped as a rainstorm blew through Spring Green the next night — a Sunday — when Mamah was buried on a family plot near Taliesin in a simple pine casket.

"The hour was hers," said a story in the State Journal. "The sermon was his. It was their last together."

Except for a single, simple pledge, Wright was quiet and contemplative during the funeral. "We will rebuild that which is home to me," he said. Within two days, the debris had been cleared away and construction began on a new Taliesin — a memorial to Mamah.

In the Iowa County Jail, Carlton still wasn't eating. He would die a few weeks later from the lingering effects of muriatic acid. He would never go to trial and his crazed attack on Mamah and the others at Taliesin never would be fully explained. Some people would say that Carlton was influenced by an evangelical minister to take action against Wright's immorality but that seems unlikely since the architect was out of town at the time of the attack.

The following week, Wright wrote a moving and lengthy tribute to Mamah, defending their adulterous affair in the Wisconsin State Journal.

"I would very much like to defend a brave and lovely woman from the pestilential torch of stories made by the press for the man in the street," he wrote.

"We have lived frankly and sincerely as we believed and we have tried to help others to live their lives according to their ideals.

"Only true love is free love — no other kind is or ever can be free. The freedom in which we joined was infinitely more difficult than any conforming with customs would have been. Few will ever venture it.

"She was struck down by a tragedy that hangs by the slender thread of reason over the lives of all, a thread which may snap at any time in any home with consequences as disastrous."

His essay ended by repeating his pledge to rebuild: "My home will still be there."

Several months after the tragedy, Wright received a condolence letter from Miriam Noel, whom he described as an "understanding stranger." A noted Parisian sculptress, she soon provided more than solace to the famous architect. She moved in with him at Taliesin and they traveled together to the Orient. But Wright remained married to Catherine, who refused to grant him a divorce.

Finally, a decade after the fatal fire that killed Mamah Borthwick, Wright won his divorce from Catherine. He and Miriam were married in a romantic ceremony at midnight on a bridge across the Wisconsin River.

But Miriam proved far less understanding than Wright imagined when the architect wanted to resume his philandering ways. In the mid-1920s, he took up with a Montenegran dancer, Olga Milanoff, and wanted to end the marriage but Miriam fought back.

Exiled from her former home, Miriam sent deputies and process servers to Taliesin but they were met by Wright's own armed guards. She even tried herself to gain access to the estate but was rebuffed. Later, she had the architect arrested in Minneapolis on a bogus violation of the Mann Act, an archaic law that prohibited sexual relations between unmarried people.

Perhaps the tragedy that summer of 1914 at Taliesin bound Wright ever more strongly to Wisconsin. If the murders and destruction hadn't occurred, he and Mamah may have moved on. Instead, he did rebuild Taliesin as a memorial to his lost lover and rebuilt the original "love bungalow" again after a second fire damaged it in 1925. The Wright home in Spring Green ensured that his designs would have a lasting influence in Wisconsin and throughout the world.

Chapter 4

The seige of Cameron Dam

Thornapple River, 1904

In mid-April 1904, loggers were poised to raise the gates on the Cameron Dam so hundreds of thousands of logs could flow downstream.

"Don't raise those gates!" John F. Dietz shouted at them. When they ignored him, he fired a single shot that whizzed close to one of the men. They stopped.

"Nobody else come close to my dam!" he warned. The single shot ignited a six-year battle between Dietz and the lumber barons. His struggle captured the public's fascination and marked the twilight of the Wisconsin frontier.

Dietz had a rather simple gripe. He believed he should be paid for the three years he spent watching the dam for the Chippewa Lumber & Boom Co. of Chippewa Falls. But the lumber company claimed Dietz was only hired for a couple weeks during the spring lumber drive.

Although the dispute was simple, its resolution was not. Dietz battled the lumber company for six years and his struggle became symbolic of a poor farmer's fight against the rich lumber barons. He singlehandedly stopped a log drive by the Midwest's biggest lumber combine. He spurned several attempts to arrest him, often sending lawmen in hasty retreat. Dietz was the last of the Wisconsin frontiersmen.

During the early years of this century, the lumber business in Wisconsin was controlled by two powerful men. Edward Hines, who owned several Great Lakes barges and a large Chicago lumber business, teamed up with Frederick Weyerhaeuser to log the dense forests of northern Wisconsin.

Dietz was born in 1861. His father, a German immigrant, fought on the union side in the Civil War and afterward, moved to Wisconsin, settling in Barron County. The Dietz family became known as "Winchester" farmers, quick to defend their property with a rifle.

In 1882, Dietz married Hattie Young, whom he called "Tatsy," and the young couple started a family. But young Dietz didn't care for farming and, by 1899, he decided to go into the real estate business with his brother. The business, however, didn't go well, although Dietz was able to acquire some property along the Thornapple River near the Cameron Dam.

In April 1901, he was approached by John Mulligan, a foreman with Chippewa Lumber & Boom. Mulligan offered Dietz a salary of $2 a day if he would keep an eye on the company's Price Dam on the Brunet River, Dietz moved his family into a shack near the dam. In 1902, he was paid $72 for 36 days of work watching the dam. Dietz claimed he had earned more. The lumber company claimed Dietz had been hired only to watch the dam during the spring drive.

In February 1904, Dietz went to see Mulligan about the additional wages. A brawl ensued and Dietz claimed he was attacked with fists and a stick by Mulligan and one of his workers.

Dietz decided to fight back. He moved his wife and six children to the Cameron Dam on the Thornapple River and, from April 10-15, 1904, he blocked the dam, holding up the lumber drive. An estimated 6.5 million feet of timber was jammed into the flowage above the dam. The blockade clearly hurt the lumber company but it took several months for them to do something about it. In July

STATE HISTORICAL SOCIETY OF WISCONSIN

John Dietz and family at the cabin.

and again in November, representatives were sent to the Dietz homestead to reach a settlement.

But the situation already was becoming more complicated. After the incident with Mulligan, it seems Mulligan swore out a complaint against Dietz and an arrest warrant was issued. The sheriff, however, was reluctant to serve the warrant.

Another complication was that Dietz learned a portion of the Cameron Dam, originally built by Thomas Leavitt and sometimes called the Leavitt Dam, was on his land. He posted a "No Trespassing" sign and told lumber company representatives a fair settlement would be payment to him of 10 cents a thousand for logs sluiced through the co-owned dam.

Two weeks after Dietz first blocked the dam, the lumber company won a court judgment for $84.12 in damages. But the judgment neglected to mention who was supposed to pay the damages.

"I won't be taken alive!" Dietz told Deputy Fred Clark, who came to serve the warrant on May 3. Two more deputies were sent out five days later but ran into an ambush Dietz had set up behind a knoll. One shot grazed a deputy's hat. The following day, a group of loggers were shot at by a sniper while they were eating dinner. A bullet broke the left arm of one logger. Dietz later wrote a poem describing the loggers scrambling for cover behind pea sacks.

By October 1904, a judge found Sheriff Peterson in contempt for failing to serve the warrant on Dietz. Peterson was sentenced to pay a $150 fine and serve 30 days in jail. Instead, he was defeated in that fall's election by James Gylland. When another deputy tried to serve the warrant in November, Dietz grabbed it out of his hands and threatened him. The deputy picked up the warrant and fled back to Hayward.

Sawyer County officials concluded they might need some help in bringing Dietz to justice. The county board passed a resolution authorizing the expenditure of $500, clearly a reward, to bring in the difficult farmer.

Early the following year, the lumber company got tired of trying to deal with local officials and got a federal court injunction that prohibited Dietz from interfering with the log drives. The injunction assessed damages at $20,000.

In early April, 1905, three men came to the Dietz homestead, claiming to be interesting in buying land. One of them returned later with a paper for Dietz. But Dietz ordered him off his property and, when the man didn't comply, the farmer hit him and physically kicked him out of the house. Dietz picked up a rifle and threatened to shoot the man but his wife stopped him. The men were Herman Jonas of Madison, Charles Callaghan of Hayward and Henry Conlin of Bayfield, acting under authority of U.S. Marshal Charles Lewiston.

With several failed attempts to snare Dietz, U.S. Marshal William Appleby decided to go a step further. He rounded up a posse of 25 men, including eleven Chicago detectives. On May 22, Appleby, Lewiston and the posse set up camp near Cameron Dam. Appleby sent a neighbor, Charles O'Hare, to the Dietz home as a peace envoy. Dietz refused to surrender and the posse departed without him, leaving the federal warrants with Sheriff Gylland.

On July 3, 1905, Gylland went to the Dietz homestead carrying a subpoena for Dietz to appear a the trial of his accomplice in the knoll ambush. Dietz hid behind the barn and Gylland failed to serve the subpoena.

Justice continued to move at a snail's pace. The following April (1906), the determined U.S. marshals tried again to serve their warrants on Dietz. The farmer confronted Deputy Marshal William Pugh and Conlin outside his home. Dietz raised a rifle and ordered them to halt. Pugh set down his papers on a pile of lumber. When the men were gone, Dietz jabbed a pitchfork into the papers and tossed them in the river.

By this time, authorities had made 10 attempts to arrest Dietz but failed each time. The case was gaining some notoriety and news-papers debated the pros and cons. Some editorialized that the state militia should be sent in to bring the scoundrel to justice; others ar-gued that the poor, crusading farmer should be left alone. Gylland tried to round up another posse but none of the locals would join. He went to Milwaukee and recuited a group of men, dressing them in National Guard uniforms to strike fear into Dietz.

When Gylland and his new posse sneaked up on the Dietz family, son Clarence was standing with a pitchfork in a load of hay. Daughter Myra was driving a team of horses while Dietz and his wife were in the barn loft, stomping down the hay. Hattie Dietz looked outside and saw a cow perk up its ears, as if at something in the bushes down by the river. She alerted the family. Dietz and his son grabbed their rifles.

"Get out of here, you sons of bitches!" Dietz shouted, then he started firing into the bushes, wounding one of the men, John Rogich, in the neck. Several men fled back to the lumber camp. Rogich picked up his gun and fired, creasing young Clarence's skull. Son Leslie and Dietz hunted down Rogich and shot him in the hip and heel.

Gylland ran to help Rogich but got stuck in the mud as a pair of bullets whizzed past his ear. Dietz and his sons retreated and Gylland was able to rescue Rogich. Swarms of deer flies and mos-quitoes attacked Rogich's wounds. Miraculously, he survived by sub-merging himself in the water. Clarence Dietz carried a scar on his head from the gun battle for the rest of his life.

The shootout at Cameron Dam fueled Dietz' popularity and

enhanced the growing legend around him. A postcard featured "the cow that served as a watchdog for Dietz." The Milwaukee Journal sponsored a poll on what should be done with the renegade farmer. Most readers said he should be left alone.

Logs continued to jam the flowage above the dam until a portion of the dam was washed away in 1906. More than a million logs were strewn everywhere, many on the Dietz property. By June 1907, officials of the lumber company had enough and decided to settle with Dietz. W.E. Moses was sent out as a representative of Frederick Weyerhaeuser. Dietz was paid $1,717 in back wages, although Dietz claimed the company owed him $8,000 by this time.

"For four long years, myself and my family have been the targets of blackmail and bullets of the land pirates and timber wolves," he said. Dietz was allowed to keep the logs that wound up on his land. A.E. Roese, editor of the Osceola Sun, also came to the farmer's aid, paying his property taxes for 1907. For awhile, Roese arranged clandestine shipments of flour, sugar, coffee and other staples so family members wouldn't have to risk coming into nearby Winter to buy necessities.

The lumber company settlement appeared to end the dispute. Dietz and his family began making regular visits to Winter for supplies, making the pipeline arranged by Roese unnecessary. For more than three years, law enforcement officials made no further efforts to arrest Dietz.

But the warrants remained on the books and local officials were as determined as ever to bring Dietz to justice. In 1907, the Sawyer County Board upped the ante to $1,000 for anyone who could bring in the fugitive.

An ironic aspect to the entire controversy was that Dietz demanded that the town board provide a teacher for his children because his homestead didn't lie within an existing school district. Despite the attempts to arrest Dietz, the town officials complied and Ethel Young, who taught during the 1905-06 school year, began the first of a succession of teachers provided to the family. In 1908, one of the Dietz children, Stanley, 8, died of pneumonia.

In 1909, on one of the family's visits to Winter, Dietz approached Dick Phelan, owner of the local hotel, and taunted him.

"Woof! Woof!" he called to Phelan. "Ain't you afraid of me?"

"Why don't you give yourself up?" Phelan suggested.

"No sirree! I'll never give myself up. They'll have to come and get me."

On Sept. 6, 1910, Dietz and his son, Clarence, went to Winter for supplies. Clarence approached Charles O'Hare, a town board member, about whether the town would assign a teacher that fall for the younger Dietz children. A fight ensued and Bert Horel, another town board member, hit John Dietz in the neck. He responding by pulling out his rifle and shooting Horel in the shoulder. The incident rekindled the ire of local officials, who agreed someone must put an end to the renegade farmer's unlawful acts.

Later that month, Sheriff Mike Madden recruited Fred Thorbahn, a Radisson shopkeeper, and Ray Van Alstine to help him arrest Dietz. Madden decided to wait for Dietz to come to Winter on one of the family's supply runs. On Saturday, Sept. 21, the three men lay in ambush for the family's wagon. As luck would have it, Dietz stayed home that day for an interview with Floyd P. Gibbons, a Minneapolis reporter. He sent Clarence, then 23, Myra, then 21, and Leslie, then 20, to town instead.

Thinking Dietz might be hiding, Madden and his men ambushed the wagon anyway. The trigger-happy Thorbahn and Van Alstine began firing. During the ensuing gunfight, Clarence was shot in the arm and Myra was hit in the stomach.

"I didn't tell them to shoot!" Madden shouted, running out of the woods. Leslie escaped but the other two Dietz children were handcuffed and arrested. Myra Dietz was rushed in a railroad baggage car to St. Joseph's Hospital in Ashland for treatment of her serious wounds. Although she survived, the incident ignited the Dietz controversy all over again. The St. Paul Dispatch editorialized that the botched arrest attempt was "a travesty of law and order." Wisconsin Gov. Davidson received 10,000 letters about the case, most of them supporting Dietz.

In the face of public outcry, the governor sent Attorney General Frank Gilbert to meet Dietz. The farmer met Gilbert's entou-

John Dietz in jail, October 1910.

rage on the banks of the Thornapple River and raised his hat.
"Can you see any horns on my head?" he asked.

Gilbert conferred with Dietz and left a letter from the governor on the kitchen table but Dietz may never have opened it. The next day, the attorney general came back. He offered to drop all charges except for the shooting of Horel. Dietz refused the offer. He said he also wanted all civil actions dropped and clear title to his land. Meanwhile, Clarence languished in jail at Hayward for his role in the Horel incident.

Fog shrouded the banks of the Thornapple on Oct. 8, 1910, when Sheriff Madden once again summoned his deputies. This time, they were assisted by a posse of neighbors grown weary of the renegade farmer's defiance of the law. The posse surrounded the homestead and Thorbahn passed a note to Dietz.

"John Dietz," the note began. "You had better surrender. It will be for the best for yourself and your family. You will be treated right and get a square deal. There is no way for you to win any other way."

The note was answered by gunfire and the battle of Cameron Dam began that day in earnest. Hattie Dietz and her children took cover on the floor as the lawmen sprayed the house with fire. More than 80 rounds were blasted into the house. Dietz ran to the barn, hoping to deflect their shots away from his family. One posse member, Oscar Harp, was fatally wounded in the mouth. Harp, who had taken cover behind a pile of lumber, was the first and only casualty of the six-year Dietz seige.

After six hours of fighting, Dietz ran back to the house about 3 p.m., hoping to bandage his wounded left hand. Mrs. Dietz persuaded her husband to surrender and Dietz came out. As Thorbahn placed handcuffs on him, Dietz said that was unnecessary.

"Oh, you don't need to put those on me," he said. "I give up. You have got my word. We surrender."

Thorbahn collected the $1,000 reward and probably split it with Van Alstine. His Radisson shop burned to the ground a few days after the arrest and Thorbahn moved to Montana, where he opened a dry goods store.

Floyd Gibbons, the aggressive Minneapolis reporter who had interviewed Dietz the day his children were ambushed, cut a telephone wire at the Hotel Winter, hoping to get a leg up on the competition. But Gibbons was taken into custody and brought to Hayward to appear before a judge for the offense. He posted bail and rushed back to Cameron Dam but missed all the action. Gibbons left the Minneapolis paper and moved to the Chicago Tribune.

The Dietz trial began May 2, 1911, in Milwaukee. Dietz, who appeared a hero to many defending his property, became an object of pity when he insisted on defending himself in court. The Minneapolis Tribune described his efforts as "pathetic." His best moment was getting Van Alstine to admit that Harp could have been killed by friendly fire from posse members. Dietz also tried to raise a key issue during his cross-examination of Attorney General Gilbert.

"Is there not a law on the state book saying that a man's home is his castle, that a man has a right to defend it at the cost of his life?"

"No," Gilbert responded. "There is no such law on the state books."

Dietz was found guilty of murdering Oscar Harp and sentenced to life in prison. In 1913, a silent film titled "The Battle of Cameron Dam" was made. The Dietz family moved to Mayville to be closer to their incarcerated patriarch. In 1914, the sentence was commuted to 25 years and, on May 12, 1921, Gov. James Blaine pardoned Dietz for all his crimes. Without the pardon, he would have been released anyway the following year.

Dietz went on the lecture circuit, doing five shows a day at the Miller Theater in Milwaukee. But his family's support for him had dwindled during the years in prison and the incarceration also had taken a toll on his health. Dietz died May 8, 1924, at age 73.

In his 1974 book, *The Battle of Cameron Dam*, Malcolm Rosholt writes about the significance of the Dietz case as a symbol of transition to the new century.

"(These were) the closing days of the American frontier," he writes. "In Wisconsin, the frontier closed on the banks of the Thornapple River."

On July 4, 1970, the village of Winter celebrated Dietz Pioneer Days. Leading the parade were Myra Dietz and her brother, John Jr.

Chapter 5

A newsboy's last delivery

Superior, 1966

V alerie Fisher, 15, couldn't figure it out. She knew her brother just wasn't that irresponsible. Sure, he was just 14. Sure, they fought sometimes like all brothers and sisters do, especially those close in age. And sure, she had to admit, sometimes she thought he was a jerk.

But if there was one thing that meant a lot to Michael, it was his paper route. She had heard him early that morning, before the sun came up, bringing up his wagon from the basement just like every Sunday morning to deliver his newspapers. The family had returned early that morning from a camping trip and Michael wanted to go out right away to finish his route but his father made him wait until just before dawn.

Their dad, who ran the Lakeview Standard Station, had been called out himself about 5 a.m. to remove cars involved in an accident. When he got back home, Michael already had left on his route.

For the past four months, Michael had been delivering the Duluth News-Tribune. For a year before that, he delivered the Superior Evening Telegram.

Now, Valerie still couldn't believe it as she found Michael's wagon with two newspaper bundles, apparently abandoned along Ogden Avenue. It looked like he'd delivered just one paper! She knew where the papers were supposed to go because most of Michael's customers had called that morning wanting to know when they'd get their papers.

With a growing mix of dread and fear gripping her stomach, she pulled the wagon down the sidewalk, finishing her brother's route. When she got home, there was still no sign of her brother. The family called the police to report him missing.

About 9 p.m. that night — 12 hours after Valerie discovered her brother's wagon — Richard Vendela and Richard Orlowski were walking along Hill Avenue, about two miles away, when they spotted something in the ditch. Hill Avenue was a rural highway with brush and trees along the roadside. They had discovered Michael's body.

His head was wrapped in a red sweatshirt. He was lying on his back, fully clothed. There was no sign he had been molested and no bruises on his body to indicate there had been a struggle. Dr. Edward G. Stock, the Douglas County coroner, said the boy had been struck in the head by a single, crushing blow to the head. He had died about 14 to 16 hours before the body was discovered and apparently was dead before the body was dumped in the ditch along Hill Avenue.

Small puncture wounds found in Michael's head and neck led to early speculation that he might have been shot but this later proved untrue. No blood stains were discovered where his wagon had been found.

"Was it an accident or was it done on purpose?" wondered Police Chief Charles Barnard. He said perhaps Michael was hit by a car and the panicked driver dumped his body. Or perhaps someone murdered him. But why?

Earlier that month, Michael had finished eighth grade at the Cathedral School and was looking forward to starting high school that fall. Besides his sister, he also had two younger brothers, Carl, 10, and Timothy, 7. He was born Dec. 23, 1951, at Fort Riley, Kan. He was an altar boy at the Cathedral of Christ the King Church.

Within a day of two after the body was found, police began to rule out an accident as a probable cause of Michael's death. A car accident, especially one that killed a pedestrian, would have left some evidence — shattered glass, tire marks. But no sign of an accident was found on Ogden Avenue anywhere near where the wagon had been discovered. Even more ominous was the fact that a single item was missing — the wire cutters used by Michael to cut the steel tape around his newspaper bundles. Could the pair of wire cutters been used as a the murder weapon?

Two days after Michael's death, the Superior Jaycees put up $250 as the first contribution to a reward fund for information leading to the arrest and conviction of the boy's killer.

"We hope that the establishing of the reward will lead to definite clues and the solution of the heinous crime committed involving the Fisher youth," the Jaycess announced.

Along with the reward, Chief Barnard issued a plea to the public to come forward with information. He urged anyone who saw Michael that morning to contact the police.

On Wednesday, the Evening Telegram upped the ante, pledging another $250 for the reward fund. The City Council chipped in $100.

"I feel the city is obligated to do all it can to capture the warped mind responsible for the crime committed," said Ald. Lloyd Frier.

Now that the police had ruled out an accident, catching Michael's killer had become a community crusade. To nearly everyone in the lakeside city, it was a shocking crime, largely because an innocent victim was killed apparently without cause. It could have been anyone.

The State Crime Lab was called in to examine Michael's clothing. A hundred members of the local Civil Defense unit planned a shoulder-to-shoulder search of an area 150 feet on each side of Hill Avenue. They hoped to find the wire cutters, now believed to be the murder weapon. If they could find the wire cutters, perhaps a fingerprint or another clue would lead to Michael's killer, they hoped.

More than 100 people responded to Barnard's plea for information. Many brought in sticks the said could be the murder weapon or rags with what could be blood stain. A paper bag full of blood-stained rags was found on a girder of the Nemadji River bridge at Second Street, just three miles from where the body was discovered. On the rags were fragments of human or animal hair and tissue.

Police hoped discovery of the paper bag was a real break in the case. But, like many of the other leads, it turned out to be a dead end. The hair and tissue was positively identified as coming from an animal.

By Thursday, the reward fund had swelled to $3,000, including a $1,000 donation by the Duluth News-Tribune. Radio stations, civic groups and businesses all contributed money to help find Michael's killer. Police began a door-to-door canvass of the area along Michael's paper route in a search for possible witnesses.

"We are going on the theory that a local person or persons are responsible for the death of Michael Fisher," said Chief Barnard.

On Friday, Greg Austreng discovered a pair of tip snips in a burning trash barrel along First Street. The cutters were examined by the Crime Lab. They were similar to the pair used by Michael but no one could make a positive identification.

Over the weekend, the reward fund surpassed $4,000 and it appeared that police finally had a major break in the difficult case. A witness said he saw Michael taken away that Sunday morning in a 1959 Chevrolet Biscayne with two men inside. The man went out on his porch to get his paper when he saw two men take Michael by the shoulder and put him in the front seat of the car. At the time, the witness thought one of the men probably was the boy's dad.

One man was described as about 5 feet 6 inches tall with a slender build, dark hair and a tan complexion. He wore blue jeans and a jean jacket. The other man stayed in the car so the witness said he didn't get a good look at him. The car was described as a two-tone, white or cream on top and orange or red on the bottom. It was polished to a bright sheen, the witness told police. He had been out of town, he said, and that's why he didn't come forward earlier.

A three-state alert — Wisconsin, Minnesota and upper Michigan — was issued for the car.

That night, police in Minocqua arrested a middle-aged man on a traffic charge. He was from Superior and was in that city on the day of Michael's murder. Police also found blood on the front seat of his car.

Superior detectives rushed across the state to Minocqua. But the car didn't match the witness' description and the man later was released. In Superior, 21 cars that did match the description were examined by police but no evidence was found.

By early July, police had received more than two dozen letters and over 1,000 calls from people offering information about the case. The crime lab found only Michael's blood on the sweatshirt wrapped around his head. No unusual particles were found on his clothing. Lab investigators officially ruled out a hit-and-run accident as the cause of his death. The case was at a dead end.

The attention of the Evening Telegram turned away from the bizarre murder of a newspaper carrier for there were other stories to cover, such as the city's first woman mail carrier and shipyard labor negotiations. A month after the murder, the paper didn't bother to run an anniversary story. But it did run a story about the capture in Chicago of Richard Speck, charged with the murder of eight nurses.

More than a quarter center after the brutal murder of Michael Fisher, the case remains unsolved. Was it a thrill killing by a pair of low-lifes out on a drunken binge? Did Michael somehow cross someone who decided to get even? Was robbery or sexual molestation a motive that somehow was thwarted? Did the killers strike again and were they ever brought to justice for another crime?

It's likely these questions about their Michael's brutal murder will remain unanswered.

Chapter 6

A near-perfect crime

Stoughton, 1983

Ruth Homberg knew something was amiss with her marriage. The loving relationship she had just a couple years earlier with her husband, Gary, had deteriorated. The palatial home they shared in the town of Dunkirk near Stoughton seemed cold to her now and the dreams they had nurtured were just a distant memory. The wife often is the last to know and Ruth had heard rumors that Gary might be having an affair with another woman.

During the summer of 1983, Ruth sometimes burst into tears on her job at Millfab in Stoughton, a business in which she and her husband shared a minority ownership. Gary Homberg also was company president.

"She was very upset with domestic problems and the way things were going at work," said her co-worker and friend, Bonnie Sampson.

On Friday night, Nov. 4, 1983, Gary and Ruth Homberg spent the evening with friends, Carlton and Kenlynn Pokrandt. They had dinner and danced at the Essen Haus, a German restaurant in Madison. Gary, a German immigrant, felt comfortable in surroundings that echoed some aspects of his native land.

The evening went better than most but didn't ease Ruth's concerns about her husband. The two couples returned to Stoughton and the Pokrandts invited the Hombergs inside their Stoughton home for a drink. When Carlton and Gary left the room for a moment, Ruth seized the opportunity. She asked Kenlynn whether she knew anything about Gary's possible involvement with another woman.

"I have to know what's going on," Ruth pleaded with her friend.

Kenlynn told Ruth she had heard rumors that Gary was having an affair with Sharon Jacobson Nordness, Ruth's daughter-in-law. Despite her suspicions, Ruth was stunned by Kenlynn's confirmation of them. To Kenlynn, Ruth looked shocked and tears welled in her eyes.

When the Hombergs arrived home, Ruth decided to confront her husband directly. While he was in the bathroom, she confronted him, demanding to know if the rumors were true. . . .

What happened next is known only to Gary Homberg. But the outing with the Pokrandts would be the last time anyone saw Ruth alive. Homberg would say later that his wife left him. Although her body never was found, a jury later convicted Homberg of murdering his wife — the first murder conviction without a body in Wisconsin history.

About 6:30 a.m. the following morning, Sharon Jacobson Nordness received a call from her lover, Gary Homberg. He told her to meet him at the Dane County Regional Airport in a half hour.

Nordness circled the parking lot twice before she spotted Homberg driving into the lot in his wife's car. Homberg parked the car in a long-term parking area, then got in Nordness' car and told her to drive him home but to take a circuitous route in getting there.

On the drive back to Stoughton, Homberg told Nordness about the confrontation he had the night before with Ruth. He told her: "Ruthie's gone and she's not coming back."

"She said she was going to call Dan Wahlin," Homberg told her. Wahlin was the majority owner of Millfab and Ruth threatened to tell Wahlin about the hundreds of thousands of dollars she knew

Gary had embezzled from the company.

Gary warned Nordness to keep Ruth's disappearance a secret because she was now an accomplice to the murder.

"You're an accessory," he told her. "If I go to jail, you go to jail."

"What are you going to do with Ruthie's body?" Sharon asked. "Throw her in the furnace?"

"You don't need to know that," he snapped. "They (the police) don't have a body. There is no body."

Gary Homberg was four years old when his father, a German shoemaker, was killed in the Allied bombing of Berlin. He went to vocational school, where he studied to be a tailor, but dreamed of seeking his fortune in America.

He emigrated to Canada, where he worked as a lumberjack. He eventually came to the United States to take a job training horses in Ohio. He joined the Air Force and was stationed at Truax Field in Madison.

Ruth Homberg

After his discharge, Homberg decided to settle in Madison, where he met and married his first wife, Sara. They divorced in 1973 and Sara blamed the breakup on Gary's devotion to his career. He had been hired as a salesman for Millfab, a wood processing company in Stoughton. In three years, Homberg was named company president.

Later, Homberg would express an intense vindictiveness toward his first wife, often referring to her as "The Pig."

After Ruth Nordness came to work at Millfab in 1975, it wasn't long before she fell in love with the company president. Like Gary Homberg, she was divorced. He had two children by his first marriage; she had three from hers. They married a year later and received 40 acres of land near Stoughton as a wedding gift from her parents.

A year before the disappearance of Ruth Homberg, the affair between Homberg and Nordness began with a simple kiss in the office. Nordness was unhappy in her marriage and began to envy Ruth Homberg's lifestyle. She could barely conceal her jealousy when she and Ruth's daughter, Roxanne, accompanied Ruth on a Florida vacation. Sharon found Gary attractive and didn't repel his advances.

By the fall of 1982, the two were lovers and often arranged a secret rendezvous at hotels in the Madison area and traveled secretly to Denver. They rented rooms at the posh Edgewater Hotel and, later, after Sharon separated from her husband, Homberg rented a condominium for her in the upscale Foxwood Hills development along Moorland Road.

Nordness wanted more than just their tawdry affair. She urged Gary to divorce Ruth or get rid of her somehow. Gary said a divorce was out of the question.

"Ruthie could nail me to the cross," he said, with information about the money he was stealing from the company.

But Gary began to fantasize about killing his wife. He became fascinated with how he could commit the perfect crime.

"It kind of intrigued him," Sharon later would say at Homberg's murder trial. "It was a challenge. He thought he could do it."

He decided the best way would be to grind up an overdose of sleeping pills and put them in a drink. When Ruth passed out, he would put her in the driver's seat of her car in the garage and turn on the engine, making her death look like a suicide.

When he actually tried the scheme, however, the plan failed because Ruth didn't pass out.

The second time, however, Homberg's plan to get rid of his wife succeeded and now all that was left was to cover up the crime. Later that Saturday, about 5 p.m., he called the police to report his wife missing, saying he was supposed to meet her for lunch and was worried when she didn't show up.

Relatives of Ruth Homberg found it odd that Gary didn't

call them to ask if they had seen Ruth before reporting her disappearance to police. And the night before, Ruth had made plans with Kenlynn Pokrandt to take Ruth's mother to lunch and a church bazaar on Saturday afternoon.

On Monday, Beverly DeGront was scheduled to make her regular visit to clean the sprawling Homberg home. Before leaving home, DeGront received a call from Sharon Nordness.

"You don't have to come and clean today," Nordness told her. "Ruth is out of town and we don't know when she'll be back."

Ruth Homberg often told the cleaning lady that she knew the house better than its occupants. When DeGront arrived to clean a week later, she couldn't help making a careful inspection.

"I was convinced in my mind that Ruth would not just leave," DeGront said later. The cleaning woman knew that Ruth was close to her parents, Art and Sally Nelson, and planned to take care of them as they grew older.

When she walked into Ruth's bathroom, DeGront said, "I was frightened. I felt like someone was with me."

But more than just an eerie feeling confirmed DeGront's suspicions that Ruth had met with foul play. The only thing missing was Ruth's jewelry, which she usually kept on a vanity. DeGront knew Ruth was very particular about her appearance and couldn't believe she would leave behind her make-up, curling iron and hair dryer.

When she looked out the window, the cleaning woman saw the ground was covered with leaves except in one area. She wondered whether Ruth was buried there. Police later checked the area but found nothing.

In 1984, Sharon Nordness was divorced from her husband. Both she and Gary now were free to marry but it would never be. Instead of enhancing their relationship, the murder became a weight upon it. Nordness began to fear Gary.

"I felt I would be harmed if I talked," she said. "Just like Ruthie was."

Sharon and Gary split up. Sharon eventually remarried but Gary left Millfab and headed west. Ruth Homberg's jewelry had been missing since her disappearance and Gary told police she must have

Gary Homberg is whisked from the Dane County Airport directly to jail (1987 photo).

taken it with her. A year later, however, Gary sold her bracelet on consignment to a Madison company and gave a gold choker to a woman in Denver.

The same year, he testified at a hearing to appoint a receiver for Ruth's property that she owned no expensive jewelry and that he made no profit from selling anything she owned. In 1987, Homberg sold the 40-acre estate on Leslie Road.

Although there was no hard evidence that Ruth Homberg had been murdered, Dane County Detective Merle Ziegler became convinced she had met with foul play. As the years went by, the inconsistencies about the case began to grow.

Ziegler and other deputies searched the Homberg estate for Ruth's body. They pumped the septic tank and also searched the grounds of the Stoughton Conservation Club and the shores of the Yahara River.

"We looked everywhere we could think of," Ziegler said. "It was an almost insurmountable task but we did our best. But we couldn't come up with anything."

By the spring of 1987, however, Ziegler had amassed circumstantial evidence that pointed to Homberg as a possible suspect. But that wasn't Homberg's only problem. In 1986, the state Department of Revenue began a probe of Millfab's finances and investigator Donald Murphy eventually uncovered evidence that Homberg embezzled more than $600,000 from the company.

A secret John Doe probe was conducted in April to gather evidence in the murder case. Among the witnesses called to testify was Sharon Jacobson Nordness, Homberg's former lover. Sharon said she knew nothing about Gary Homberg's possible murder of his wife.

Without any physcial evidence and with Sharon's testimony, the murder case against Homberg remained weak. But the embezzlement case was stronger. Days after the John Doe investigation ended, papers were filed to extradite Homberg from California to face tax fraud and embezzlement charges in Madison. At the time, Homberg was managing a lumberyard in Fontana, earning an annual salary of $100,000.

The lengthy investigation had discovered that Homberg, between 1982 and 1986, issued himself 48 Millfab checks ranging in amounts from under $2,000 to more than $27,000, then disguised the checks in the company's record books as payments to suppliers from the raw materials account. The embezzlement of more than $600,000 helped Ruth and Gary Homberg finance their extravagent lifestyle.

"No wonder the company was broke," said a shocked Dan Wahlin when he learned of the massive embezzlement scheme.

Ruth Homberg's son, Richard Nordness, was pleased that his ex-stepfather and ex-wife's lover finally was in custody.

"At last, maybe we can get some answers," he said.

Richard Nordness had known about his wife's affair with Gary long before his mother found out about it. He had discovered a letter from Gary to Sharon in his wife's purse, extolling her virtues as a lover.

Homberg was jailed on $300,000 cash bail until the amount was lowered several months later and he was permitted by the court to resume his job managing the lumberyard.

By the end of the year, Homberg pleaded no contest to reduced charges of two counts of embezzlement and two counts of tax fraud involving about $245,000 in company funds. Dane County Judge Robert Pekowsky ordered a pre-sentence review and allowed Homberg to remain free on bond. With the convictions, he faced fines up to $40,000 and 30 years in prison.

Homberg was sentenced to seven years in prison on the embezzlement and fraud convictions and he returned to Wisconsin. Police finally had Homberg cold on the embezzlement but Ziegler wondered whether he would ever come to trial for the murder of his wife. He conferred with veteran prosecutor John Burr. How could they charge him with murder without a body? It was unprecedented.

Yet Ziegler and other sheriff's investigators had done everything humanly possible to find Ruth Homberg's remains. One thing the detective was sure of: She definitely was no longer alive.

By spring, however, a major break in the case caused Ziegler and Burr to bring Homberg to trial even without a body. Sharon Jacobson Nordness had agreed to talk under a grant of immunity from prosecution. Despite her earlier lies to the John Doe grand jury, now she changed her story about her ride with Homberg back to Stoughton that Saturday morning.

"He said something to the effect that he killed her and that she wasn't coming back, that it happened quickly," Nordness testified at a preliminary hearing. Homberg was charged with first-degree murder and held on $100,000 bail.

It would be more than a year, however, before the case came to trial in October 1989. Prosecutors offered Homberg a deal, saying they would reduce the charge if he pleaded guilty. "I didn't do it," he replied.

In January 1989, assistant public defender Dennis Burke moved for dismissal of the murder charges against Homberg. Burke charged prosecutors with unreasonable delays in providing him with evidence about the case. He said seven months had passed since the district attorney's office agreed to provide more than 3,500 pages of police reports about the case.

As expected, a key witness at the trial was Sharon Jacobson Nordness. She described her ride with Homberg and the events on that Saturday morning. During cross-examination, however, Burke launched a severe attack on her credibility, pointing out that her testimony was inconsistent with earlier testimony she had given about the case.

Other important witnesses included Ziegler, Richard Nordness and cleaning woman Beverly DeGront.

To refute Sharon's testimony, Burke called Gary Lintvedt, who dated her during the summer of 1984 when she was breaking off her relationship with Homberg. Lintvedt said she never expressed any fears of Gary.

Lintvedt said he had heard that Ruth Homberg once walked in to discover Gary and Sharon in bed together. But Lintvedt said he couldn't recall whether Sharon had told him that or whether it was a rumor he had heard.

Prosecutor John Burr also brought out the inconsistencies in Homberg's behavior concerning his wife's jewelry and in reporting her disappearance. Witnesses were asked if they saw Ruth Homberg at the funerals of her parents, who died in 1988.

But the state's case clearly rested on the testimony of Sharon Jacobson Nordness. Prosecutors could offer absolutely no physical evidence. There were no hairs or fibers linking Homberg to his wife's murder and, without a body, some doubt remained about whether she actually had been killed.

Would the jury believe Sharon's story? Or would they give weight to Burke's argument that she had lied before about the case. Burke decided not to call Homberg to testify in his own defense.

In the end, the testimony was enough for the jury to convict

Homberg of first degree murder in the unprecedented case and he was sentenced to life imprisonment.

Despite the conviction, a major loose end remained. Judge Gerald Nichol offered to reduce Homberg's sentence if he revealed the location of Ruth's body.

"I haven't killed Ruthie and I haven't killed anyone else," Homberg told the judge. "How can a person show remorse when he hasn't done anything wrong?"

Two years later, the Appeals Court upheld the conviction, ruling that "the jury heard overwhelming evidence that Homberg intended to get rid of his wife, and that he did."

If the jury's decision was correct, Gary Homberg had dreamed about commiting the perfect crime. He had planned how to kill his wife and dispose of her body where no one would find it, But the flaw in his perfect scheme came when he had to dispose of her quickly and in his failure to cover up the crime. Many Stoughton residents believe Ruth's body ended up in the furnace at Millfab, capable of generating heat of more than 2,500 degrees.

What became of Ruth Homberg's body? Does Gary Homberg have the answer?

Chapter 7

Fatal attraction for a dairy princess
Wausau, 1989

S uccess seemed to come easily to Lori Esker. She was class president at Wittenberg-Birnamwood High School. Growing up in rural Hatley, about 25 miles east of Wausau, she also served as president of the high school chapter of Future Farmers of America. She was a member of the National Honor Society and a runner on the girls' track team. Pretty and smart, young Lori was as popular with administrators and teachers as she was with fellow students. For three years, she held a part-time job in the school office.

After high school, she enrolled at the University of Wisconsin-River Falls. In June 1989, everything seemed to be going right for Lori. She won the title of Marathon County dairy princess and was making plans to marry Bill Buss, a tall, strong, dark-haired and handsome Wausau-area farmer. Her college friends said she talked constantly about Bill and often window-shopped for a wedding dress. Lori told her friends they were engaged, although she never showed them a ring.

"I would say that she was bright, articulate, competent and a very attractive girl," said Jean Flefson, her faculty advisor. Lori and

Bill were business partners, too, because Bill kept 17 head of cattle Lori owned at his farm. Lori no doubt viewed this arrangement as a prelude to their marriage, when all of their possessions would be comingled.

The way Buss viewed his relationship with Lori, however, was far different than her fantasies of marriage and family. And on June 23, when he told her he wanted to end the relationship because he was getting back together with his long-time girlfriend, Lisa Cibaski, it would unleash a chain of events resulting in Lisa's violent death. Buss was unaware that Lori apparently had become obsessed with him in a fatal attraction.

Buss and Cibaski dated for about three years before she decided to cool the relationship, telling him she needed "some space." Buss began dating Esker but, by January 1989, he felt the romance with the dairy princess beginning to sour. He renewed his acquaintance with Cibaski and they talked on the phone more than a dozen times before that fateful June night, when he took Esker to a street dance and told her their relationship was over.

Lori was devastated. The end of her relationship with Buss set her emotions on a roller coaster. She hated him but she loved him. Her friend, Tammy Zack, tried to console her.

"She just didn't want to break up," Zack said. "Sometimes she cried."

Lori wasn't used to losing and she wasn't about to give up her man that easily. Twice, she visited Buss after his midnight milking chores, stripping off her clothes and climbing into his bed dressed only in a skimpy nightgown. She called him frequently and once reached him at a friend's house.

"How could you do this to me?" she cried. He hung up on her. She called Alan Andrus, a friend of Bill's, and pleaded with him to intercede and help get them back together. "I could just kill her," she said of Lisa. "Just kill her."

That summer was miserable for the dairy princess. As the weeks went by, her obsession only deepened. Her friends noticed that the Lori they knew — the intelligent, well-rounded Lori with diverse interests — could focus only on her lost boyfriend and how to win

Lori Esker, former Marathon County dairy princess.

him back. In September, someone told Lori that Lisa was pregnant and that rumor may have been what finally set her on course to murder. The pregnancy, if true, could put Buss out of reach. Even worse, it would be concrete evidence of his relationship with Lisa.

Lori called Buss to confront him about Lisa's pregnancy. He

denied it, telling her the rumor was false. During the conversation, he mentioned that Lisa would be working late on the night of Sept. 20.

"I just want you to know that I have accepted the fact that Lisa and you are back together and I am going to leave you alone now," Lori told him. But it was a lie.

On Sept. 20, Lori left this message on a friend's answering machine: "Hi. This is Lori. I am going to the library. Maybe I will talk to you later." Then, she got in her car and drove 150 miles from River Falls to Wausau. She later told detectives she came to Wausau "to get things straightened out."

Lisa Cibaski

Knowing that Cibaski was working late, Lori drove to the Howard Johnson's Motor Lodge in Rib Mountain, where Lisa held a job as assistant sales and catering manager. They got into Cibaski's car to talk. When Lori asked her about being pregnant, their conversation grew more heated.

"I thought she was going to kill me or really hurt me," Lori later told investigators. She reached into the back seat of Cibaski's car and grabbed a belt, wrapping it around her neck.

"I pushed on her," Lori later said. "I don't know if it was the belt or my elbow."

When Cibaski passed out, Lori began to panic. She grabbed Cibaski's purse and pulled out a mirror. She held it to the other woman's face to see if she was still breathing.

"Oh, my God!" Lori said to herself. "I killed her."

Lisa Cibaski's body was found the next morning by her mother, Shirley, who had become worried that her daughter was missing. The body was found in Lisa's parked car, where Lori had left her.

It didn't take investigators too long to figure out who might have wanted Lisa Cibaski dead and, eight days after the murder, Lori was arrested. She made her initial appearance in Marathon County Circuit Court Oct. 2 on a charge of first-degree intentional homicide.

Although they were aware of Lori's obsession with Bill Buss, her friends at UW-River Falls were shocked that she would be accused of killing her romantic rival. It certainly was out of character for the bright, articulate dairy princess. Counselors worked with students to help them cope with the emotional stress of their classmate's crime.

Bill Buss

Esker agreed to take a lie detector test and then, with the encouragement of Bill Buss, she confessed to the crime. It was a confession that her attorney, Stephen Glynn, later would claim was coerced.

"You were playing her the way a violinist would play a fiddle, working her for every bit of information you could get," Glynn told District Attorney Greg Grau, while arguing a motion to dismiss the murder charge at a pretrial hearing. The motion was denied.

At the trial in early June 1990, friends of Lori testified about her obsession with Buss and refusal to give up the affair. Buss testified in a hushed courtroom for about 90 minutes, giving details of their affair and Lori's subsequent efforts to get back together after he broke it off.

The case centered on whether Lori plotted to kill Lisa, a necessary element for conviction of first-degree murder. Glynn argued the killing occurred in a moment of passion. Grau said Lori's message on the answering machine indicated the murder was pre-meditated.

On June 15, 1990, jurors deliberated for more than seven hours before finding Lori guilty of first degree murder. Members of the Cibaski family reacted with glee, hugging each other and shouting "Yes! Yes!" outside the courtroom.

"She always had to be number one and she got number one," said Vilas Cibaski, Lisa's father.

But Bill Buss wasn't joyful about the verdict.

"My life will never return to normal because Lisa will never be back," he said.

At her sentencing hearing, Lori pleaded for leniency, saying she was "so sorry" for all the pain and suffering she caused.

"If I could trade places with Lisa, I would in a minute," she said, asking for a "chance to start paying back all the people I hurt so bad.

"I will be punishing myself for as long as I live. There isn't a day that goes by that I don't think about what happened."

It was ironic that Lori also had wanted to trade places with Lisa a year earlier and, in fact, that's what drove her to kill.

Judge Michael Hoover sentenced Lori Esker to life in prison but, due to her clear criminal record, he made her eligible for parole in 13 instead of 20 years.

"It's as much a tragedy that has befallen the defendant's family as the Cibaski family," the judge said. "No one expects the Cibaski family to understand that, at least not today. I know this sentence leaves them wholly unsatisfied and perhaps that much farther away from healing."

Lori Esker killed for love. But that motive and the judge's sympathy were little comfort to the Cibaskis, who lost their daughter to a jealous killer.

"Lori Esker took something very precious from me," Shirley

Cibaski testified at Lori's sentencing hearing. "She took something and destroyed it and it can never be replaced."

While the deep wound to the Cibaski family left by Lisa's death may never fully heal, Bill Buss at least has been able to move on with his life. In early 1993, he announced his engagement to Linda Gritzmacher, a Wausau legal secretary with a 5-year-old son. Buss continues to operate his 440-acre farm and tends 54 head of cattle.

"It's not totally behind me," he said. Perhaps it never will be.

Chapter 8

A spinster's revenge
Waukesha, 1917

The fatal love triangle involving the dairy princess wasn't Wisconsin's first, nor last, crime of passion. A similar case involving a love triangle ended the same way on a spring day in 1917 in Waukesha — with a woman killing her rival for a man's affections.

On a warm day in May that year, Grace Lusk sat at her writing desk, trying to compose a letter to Mary Newman Roberts. The act of writing itself wasn't a problem, for Grace Lusk was a brilliant school teacher. But the deep passions involved made the words come hard.

"It has been a desire with me for a long time," she began, "to tell you frankly about the state of affairs between Dr. Roberts and myself. I have asked him repeatedly to tell you the whole story, but you seem to have him terrorized to a pitiful degree. If I have to blame you for one thing, it would be for that. You must have known for many years that there did not exist between your husband and yourself the honest confidence that is essential in the higher state of marriage."

It was a brave letter for Grace Lusk but, after all, she was nearing the end of her rope. She had met David Roberts four years earlier at a party in the home of Mrs. S.B. Mills. Roberts, in his 50s, ran the David Roberts Veterinary Co., which manufactured cattle preparations and other animal medications. He also operated a dairy and breeding farm.

Grace Lusk was in her 30s and, in her era, she was nearing the end of her marriageable age. She had been teaching since she was 19. Her first principal in Menominee Falls described her as "wonderfully mature in mental attainments and a splendid teacher, a most loyal friend, a young woman of pure and noble character, a brilliant girl." She had attended the teachers' colleges known then as Milwaukee Normal and Whitewater Normal. She left her teaching job in Menominee Falls for a job in Waukesha. As part of her duties as a Waukesha teacher, Grace was required to teach agriculture, a subject she didn't know much about.

Despite her brilliance as a teacher, Grace Lusk never had taken the time to learn much of practical value, especially in relationships between men and women.

At the party, she asked Dr. Roberts about how to distinguish among various breeds of cattle. He gave her one of his books on the subject and recruited her to help him write a veterinary book. Perhaps across the desk after a long night's work, he stole a kiss or two. As part of the seduction, he told her his wife no longer loved him and Grace, inexperienced, was easily seduced.

For four years, David Roberts told Grace repeatedly that he loved her but he couldn't leave his wife. Despite what she perceived as his weakness in this area, Grace still loved him and, now, had decided to matters into her own hands with her letter.

"You must have known," she wrote, "for a long time that your husband's affections had passed from you; that he cared for someone else. That is sufficient annulment of any marriage vow that ever was given."

Despite what many of her contemporaries would call a tawdry affair, Grace had assumed the high moral ground. She was having an affair with a married man, yet it was justified because of her lover's failing marriage. Now, she grew poetic about her situation:

"That is the way you respectable folk — good, normal women — do things in order to keep your reputation and live lives of ease," she went on. "In the eternal triangle our souls require for their solution the elimination of one character. The two who should remain are the two whose affection is mutual. There is no use in my telling the details of our 'case.' I am sorry that it even started. It has wrecked my life and hurt those who are dear to me. Will you some time read Ellen Kay on *Love and Marriage*?"

Ever the teacher, Grace Lusk could not resist suggesting some reading material for her rival. Regrets? Of course she had them. For like Lori Esker, Grace Lusk was out of control. She was obsessed with her doctor lover so much that her passions clouded her very capable mind.

But unlike Bill Buss, the target of Lori Esker's affection, David Roberts wasn't an innocent party in this love triangle. He clearly had taken unfair advantage of Grace's inexperience in the ways of love. He had no intention of leaving his wife or marrying Grace as she wistfully dreamed. He was too comfortable with his wife at home and a doting mistress on the side.

David and Grace had arranged their clandestine love trysts at locations away from Waukesha, where a mutual acquaintance might discover them. They often traveled south to Illinois, finding out-of-the-way hotels in Peoria or Chicago. David had managed to make lame excuses to his wife for his absences.

When the lovers met in mid-May at the Hotel Wisconsin in Milwaukee, Grace told David about the letter. In desperation, she also brought along a revolver.

"Never in my life have I done anything which even bordered on unconventionality," she told Dr. Roberts, "and this episode has almost killed me."

Grace demanded more from David. She demanded that he tell his wife everything and leave her. Grace tied herself to the writing desk and pulled out her revolver. She pointed it at David and made him swear on the Bible that he would confess to his wife.

Of course, at that moment, David agreed. Later, after they

had made love, he hedged a bit. He told Grace he couldn't tell his wife right away because they were leaving the next day on a business trip. Maybe after that. . . Grace said she would give him until June 15.

"I want you to ask her for your freedom, David. I want you to arrange this so we can all understand each other."

The letter Grace sent to Mrs. Roberts might have created a serious problem for David if he hadn't been such an expert philanderer. He merely told his wife that the letter was from a woman who was pursing him relentlessly and making a nuisance of herself. But Mrs. Roberts wasn't totally convinced. Grace seemed to offer too many details in her letter. During the trip, Mrs. Roberts decided she must speak to this woman in person to find out the truth.

An hour after David and Mary Roberts arrived home from their trip, Grace appeared at the door. Mary Roberts encouraged her to come in but her husband quickly pushed Grace back outside and walked her home. The next morning, Mrs. Roberts called Grace and arranged to meet at her school office.

Naturally, David Roberts was upset about the idea of his wife and mistress getting together. Comparing notes by them could only be dangerous for him. He tried to talk Mary out of it and, when that failed, he cut the telephone lines to his house so his wife couldn't call Grace.

Although she didn't keep the appointment, Mary Roberts remained determined to confront her husband's pursuer. On June 21, she walked over to Mills House, a rooming house where Grace lived. Grace came downstairs to meet her in the lobby.

"I came here to get an explanation of your conduct last night," Mrs. Roberts began. "I think it was the most asinine performance I ever saw."

Grace swallowed hard but didn't respond so Mrs. Roberts went on.

"He said you are the damndest fool he ever saw. He said that you were actually chasing him, that he did not care anything about you."

"You don't mean that he said that, do you?" Grace was getting upset now.

"What else could you expect when you chase a married man?"

Mrs. Roberts demanded that Grace get out of town. She threatened to go to the school board and try to get her fired.

"My friends will put you out of town," she threatened. "They will tar and feather you!"

Mrs. Roberts demanded that Grace break off the affair with her husband. Grace, of course, refused, saying that she was David's true love. Grace said she would prove it, too. She said she would go upstairs and get the love letters from David to show Mrs. Roberts.

While Grace was getting the letters, Mrs. Roberts called her husband, asking him to come over and verify one story or the other.

Upstairs, Grace opened a dresser drawer. Instead of letters, her eyes fell on her revolver.

David Roberts reluctantly obeyed his wife's request. Earlier, he had asked a business partner to watch his house so he knew already that Mary had gone to see Grace. He and the partner, W.D. Blott, drove over to the Mills House. He was terrified. Despite his best efforts to keep them apart, the two women had gotten together. What if they compared notes and decided to turn on him? As he approached Mills House, he was too nervous to stop and drove on by. He came around the block and, on the second pass, he heard a shot.

David stopped the car and asked Blott to go take a look. Blott peeked in a window. He saw Mary Roberts lying on the floor with blood staining her side. He saw Grace coming down the stairs. Instead of bothering to check on his wife or Grace, David fled to a phone some distance away. He called the police and Dr. R.E. Davies.

When Davies arrived, he saw that Mary Roberts had been shot twice. Grace stood at the top of the stairs, bleeding from a self-inflicted wound to her chest. Davies started up the stairs.

"If you come up, I'll shoot!" Grace warned. "Where's David?"

David, of course, was still too frightened to go anywhere near the place.

"Where's my heart?" Grace wanted to know.

"What?"

"Where's my heart?"

"Why, right here," the doctor said, placing his hand over his chest. "You'd better let me tend to that wound."

Without a reply, Grace turned and went into the bedroom. Davies heard another shot and bounded up the stairs. Grace had shot herself once again in the chest and passed out. But once again she had missed her vital organs. As she was carried out on a stretcher, she regained consciousness.

"That was the most unfortunate miss I ever made," she mumbled, referring to her last shot.

At her trial, Grace's attorneys tried to portray her as neurotic and caught in the grip of an uncontrollable passion. They presented evidence that she had frequent migraine headaches and often worked too hard. They brought witnesses who said her father sometimes swatted flies away from his face in the winter and talked to his hat. Her father testified that her mother once tried to hurl herself into Niagara Falls. But three alienists, predecessors to today's forensic psychiatrists, examined Grace and found her sane.

When the guilty verdict was returned on May 29, 1918, Grace found it hard to bear. She jumped out of her chair and grabbed prosecutor D.S. Tullar around the neck in a choke hold. Several spectators, clearly sympathetic to the defendant, tried to vault the rail to help. Grace was hauled out of the courtroom shrieking as the judge rapped his gavel and restored order.

On June 18, almost exactly a year after the murder of Mary Roberts, Grace was sentenced to 19 years in prison. She also was sentenced to spend every June 21 in solitary confinement so she might reflect on her awful deed.

But Judge Martin Lueck didn't view Grace as the only culprit in the case.

"I want to say that I have one regret, a sincere regret, that I cannot mete out to Dr. Roberts the punishment I think he ought to have."

Dr. Roberts served a brief term in the Milwaukee County House of Corrections after he was convicted on a morals charge for his affair with Grace. He later remarried, proving that even the worst philanderers sometimes land on their feet.

Grace Lusk didn't recover as well as her lover from the ordeal. She was paroled in 1921 and went straight into a sanitorium at Oconomowoc. When she was pardoned two years later by Gov. John J. Blaine, she vowed to devote the rest of her life to prison reform. When Atlantic Monthly carried an article on prison reform written by an "Alice Thornton," many people assumed the author was Grace.

A few years later, Grace claimed to have married a "Mr. Brown" but no one ever saw him and some people thought he was a figment of her imagination, although she once bought some furniture and had it shipped somewhere in the South. She died in Milwaukee, still apparently alone, in 1930.

Did she ever wonder in her later years what might have been? Did she ever think about David Roberts and imagine what might have happened if Mary Roberts had taken her letter to heart and surrendered her husband? We'll never know.

Chapter 9

The Keating gang

Menomonie, 1931

B ank robberies have been an important part of Wisconsin's criminal history. In recent years, many robberies have been committed by perpetrators who were mentally unbalanced or addicted to
drugs. It takes a certain amount of moxy or irrationality to know that
you'll be photographed by bank cameras and probably identified
within a short period of time.

Latter-day robbers try disguises to fool the cameras or schemes
that prove ingenious for awhile. One of the more enterprising robbers of the 1980s would fly into Milwaukee's Mitchell Field and rent
a car. He would drive out to a small town, rob the bank, return the
car and fly back to his home in California. Inevitably he was caught,
like most contemporary bank bandits.

It wasn't always the case, however, that a bank robber was
likely to be captured. During the Depression years, banks seemed a
source of easy money for roving gangs. The most famous of these was
the John Dillinger gang. Dillinger stirred the public's fancy with his
Robin Hood antics, often vaulting bank counters and showing special consideration for customers. Dillinger robbed only a few Wis-

consin banks and his most famous exploits in that state concerned the shootout at Little Bohemia, where several innocent people were killed or wounded by FBI bullets.

Francis Keating wasn't such a gentleman bandit. In fact, his gang's holdup of the Kraft State Bank in Menomonie in 1931 was among the bloodiest in the Wisconsin history.

Keating was a Chicago hoodlum sentenced to 25 years in Leavenworth Prison for a mail robbery that netted $135,000. He and his sidekick, Tommy Holden, escaped in February 1930 using stolen trustee passes supplied to them by none other than George "Machine Gun" Kelly, a notorious bank robber later convicted of the sensational kidnapping of Oklahoma oil magnate Charles Urschell.

Chicago was crawling with gangs so Keating and Holden decided to seek their fortune, quite literally, in the Twin Cities. They selected their gang members carefully, seeking the craziest partners in crime they could find.

The most prominent member may have been Alvin "Creepy" Karpis, later captured by J. Edgar Hoover in New Orleans. After a few years with the Keating-Holden gang, Karpis went on to found his own outfit with Freddie Barker, another Keating-Holden robber, and Freddie's mother, known as Ma Barker. Another notorious member included Frank "Jelly" Nash, later gunned down in Kansas City.

None of these characters were along Oct. 20, 1931, when the Keating-Holden gang descended on the Kraft State Bank shortly after it opened. Two bandits entered the bank while a third stood guard outside with a sub-machine gun, liberally firing up and down the street to keep away anyone who sought to interfere.

The two gunman inside ordered 10 bank employees and four customers to lie on the floor while they scooped up all the available cash in the tellers' cages. After cleaning out the cash drawers, the bandits demanded more money from owner William F. Kraft. When he said there wasn't any more money, one of the cold-blooded robbers fired at Kraft's son with a .45-caliber revolver, wounding him in the shoulder. The bandits grabbed a female bank teller, hoping to use her as a shield so they could reach their getaway car.

Outside, a crowd began to gather despite the gunman's ef

forts to keep them away. In the excitement, the teller escaped but James Kraft, the owner's son, was forced into a getaway car. As the bandits drove off with a haul of about $7,000, Ed Kinkle, a citizen, fired at the fleeing auto. One of his bullets went through the rear window.

Kinkle said later he must have scored a direct hit on one of the bandits because he heard someone yell, "Ouch!" In fact, Krinkle's shot probably killed robber Frank Webber of Minneapolis, whose body was thrown from the car about eight miles from Menomonie. Webber, 33, was a Wisconsin native who served time at a Salt Lake City prison for bank robbery. As retribution for killing one of their gang, the gunmen murdered James Kraft, 19, and also flung his body out of the car on the road to Wheeler.

Vernon Townsend, a bank guard, also fired at the getaway car from the roof of the building. Townsend watched the entire robbery from his station above the teller cages but claimed he was under strict orders not to shoot inside the bank. He sounded the burglar alarm, then crawled to the roof. One of his shots hit the car's gas tank.

The gunmen headed north, through Wheeler, Boyceville, Prairie Farm and on toward Clear Lake. When word of James Kraft's murder reached Menomonie, hundreds of angry citizens grabbed guns and took off in pursuit of the killers.

Margaret King reported spotting the gunmen near her family's farm north of Menomonie:

"I was hunting in the woods near home when I saw three men in a car parked along the road. I thought they were hunters and one of them had been shot because the other two were bandaging him.

"I kept out of sight but I noticed that the windshield of the car was broken and that there were bullet holes in it."

The King farm had no phone and hadn't heard of the robbery when Margaret spotted the men.

The brutal robbers pressed on, zig-zagging across northern Wisconsin. A third body was found near Shell Lake. He was identified as Preston Harmon of Texas. He served time in a Texas prison for holding up a poker game and also was at Leavenworth with Francis

Keating for robbing the post office at Davenport, Iowa. Buckshot lodged in Harmon's body indicated the gun fight outside the Kraft State Bank wasn't his first. A machine gun and two pistols believed used in the robbery were found near Harmon's body.

An airplane was brought in from Eau Claire to search the woodlands. Circling over the isolated lake shores, the plane found no sign of the bandits. On the ground, posses from six counties armed with rifles, shotguns and pitchforks kept watch along main highways. The citizen army found the abandoned getaway car about six miles east of Webster. Bullets had shattered its rear window and blood was found on the back seat.

Sheriff Ike Harmon, no relation to the dead bandit, reported his deputies were near collapse after working long hours to track the bandits. The trail led back into Minnesota as the bandits were spotted crossing the border near Markman and heading for Sandstone.

As part of the investigation, detectives questioned Babe White, a Chicago man who called himself "the human fly." White was seized and handcuffed in Portage, in front of a crowd of several hundred spectators gathered to watch him scale the Raulf Hotel.

White, who climbed the Marion Hotel in Menomonie the night before the robbery, was seen shaking hands with Frank Webber before the performance. But White said he wasn't acquainted with Webber.

"I thought that man was a Swedish singer, one of a show troupe whose act at a Menomonie theater was to have been announced by me during my ascent," White said.

The Kraft robbery was only the beginning of the Keating-Holden gang's reign of terror. Keating quickly recruited new members to replace the dead men and the gang was linked to robberies at Colfax, Cumberland and Duluth, Minn. Investigators gave up the search for the Kraft bandits after three weeks.

Unlike Dillinger and many other bank robbers of the era, Keating and Holden didn't die in a flash of gunfire. They were arrested by FBI agents on July 7, 1932, along with accomplice Harvey Bailey, while playing golf at the Old Mission Golf Course in Kansas City.

The agents didn't realize that a fourth golfer was part of the group. Frank "Jelly" Nash was such a terrible golfer and trailed so far behind his three comrades that he avoided capture. The capture ended the criminal careers of Keating and Holden, who spent the rest of their lives in prison.

But Nash wouldn't always be so lucky. Less than a year later, he died during a shootout with federal agents known as the Kansas City Massacre. Besides Nash, four agents were killed and two were wounded. The shootout on June 17, 1933, occurred in an attempt to free Nash, who had been captured in Hot Springs, Ark. and was being transferred to Kansas City, Mo. Among the gangster machine gunners was the legendary "Pretty Boy" Floyd.

Chapter 10

A Halloween outrage

Fond du Lac, 1973

No crime enrages a community more than the murder or sexual assault of a child. These crimes against children violate a trust that forms one of the major underpinnings of our society. When a perpetrator is caught and jailed, other prisoners often treat him with contempt. If a modern-day lynching ever occurs, the victim probably will be one of these criminals.

Several of these cases have plagued Wisconsin throughout the century. In 1911, Madison residents were outraged by the abduction and murder of 7-year-old Annie Lemberger. The 1953 disappearance of Evelyn Hartley from her babysitting job in La Crosse has never been solved. In 1982, the brutal sexual assault and murder of Paula McCormick, 9, prompted some in the Madison community to call for the release of suspect Roger Lange so street justice could deal with him.

A similar case occurred in 1973 in Fond du Lac. Nine-year-old Lisa French put on a black felt hat and green parka. She put tape on her blue jeans before going outside. It was Halloween night and Lisa had decided to go trick-or-treating as a hobo. When she walked out the door of her Amory Street home about 5:45 p.m. that day, it was the last time her mother would ever seen Lisa alive.

About an hour later, the brown-haired fourth-grader stopped at the home of Karen Bauknect, a former teacher. Lisa made her way alone through the neighborhood, going up and down each block and collecting her bag of treats.

Not far from where Lisa was trick-or-treating, a woman, Arlene Penn, stopped home about 7 p.m. to pick up her live-in boyfriend, Gerald Turner. They were supposed to go to her mother's house. Turner met her at the door and told her he wasn't feeling well, that she should catch a ride with friends and go ahead with her daughter.

But when Penn got to her mother's house about 15 minutes later, she remembered that her mother wouldn't be home until 8 p.m. She went back to her own house. Turner, still wearing his work clothes, sat with her on the couch. He mentioned a couple of times that he felt sick and went into the bedroom to lie down.

Penn left again before 8 p.m. and didn't get home until after 11 p.m. When she arrived, Turner was dressed in a bathrobe. She noticed their green bedspread was on the floor of the laundry room and asked him about it. He said he had thrown up on it.

When Lisa failed to return home that night, her mother called the police. A massive search was mounted the following day. More than 700 block parents throughout the city were mobilized. They were assisted by Girl Scouts and auxiliary police officers summoned to duty. They checked bushes, garages and wooded areas but found no sign of the missing girl. An estimated 5,000 people participated.

By Nov. 2, Police Chief Harold Rautenberg had lost hope that Lisa would be found alive.

"I am satisfied in my own mind that she is not missing voluntarily," he told reporters. "I had that hope. Now, we have to face reality."

Just before noon on Saturday, three days after Lisa disappeared, farmer Gerald Braun was driving his tractor back to his farm along a country road in the town of Taycheedah when he spotted a brown plastic bag behind a barbed-wire fence at the edge of the woods. After parking the tractor at the farm, he returned to investigate. Inside the bag, he discovered clothing that appeared to belong to a child. In a second bag nearby was the body of Lisa French.

An autopsy determined that Lisa probably had died of suffocation. The coroner also found that she had been sexually molested.

Lisa French was buried on Nov. 6 and, at the funeral, the Rev. Paul Piotter appealed to the killer to confess.

"It is your only hope," he said. "Otherwise, you will be tormented for the rest of your days."

Piotter also blamed the crime on a permissive society that fosters conditions for it to occur.

On Nov. 8, just a week after that fateful Halloween night, the chamber of commerce offered a $10,000 reward for the capture of Lisa's killer.

"We promote Fond du Lac as an ideal place to live and work and we wish to prove what we say is true," said chamber president Louis Lange. "We want to bring this person to justice quickly."

But there would be no quick resolution to this difficult and heart-breaking case. A 25-year-old Fond du Lac man was arrested in Madison for contributing to the delinquency of a boy. He was quizzed about the Lisa French case but no connection was found.

Under community pressure to find the killer, Fond du Lac County Sheriff John Cearns assigned six full-time investigators to the case. The detectives consulted psychiatrists at Waupun state prison to put together a psychological profile of the murderer.

Cearns tried to keep most of his investigation under wraps. "If we don't talk about what we are doing," he said, "maybe we can throw the guy off guard."

Due to the lack of any sign of a struggle, the investigators believed Lisa probably knew her assailant and trusted him.

"There were no bruise marks on her," Cearns said. "You'd think that if a stranger tried to accost her, she'd scratch or claw or bite or kick. She'd have struggled.

"You've got to figure that the only person she would not do that to was somebody she had previous contact with, somebody she trusted."

Detectives developed a list of about a dozen suspects. In the

Gerald Turner

spring, the chamber of commerce added more than $2,000 to the reward but still it brought no hard information. As summer came and the investigation wore on, Gerald Turner, who worked as a railroad machinist, rose to the top of the list of suspects. He lived close to where Lisa was last seen alive and he knew her.

Before moving a few blocks away, Turner had lived next door to Lisa on Amory Street. She seemed to like him, often bringing him things to show him. In early August, Turner was arrested and charged with first-degree murder in the death of Lisa French.

While Turner was held on $100,000 bond, he made a full confession. He told investigators how he had become sexually aroused when Lisa came to the door that night. He sexually assaulted her but then something went wrong and the girl died. He described how he had put her body and clothing in separate garbage bags and dumped the bags at Braun's farm. Turner said he didn't tell Penn anything about the girl's death due to "fear of apprehension for the murder and sexual molestation of a young girl."

After intense questioning by Louis Tomaselli of the state Division of Criminal Investigation and Rodney Anderson of the state Crime Lab, Turner signed each page of the typed confessions and carefully initialed corrections.

Turner pleaded innocent to the murder and sexual perversion charges. The week before the trial began in late January 1975, he dropped a plea of innocent by reason of mental disease after receiving a psychiatrist's report that found him sane.

Using a combination of witnesses and scientific evidence, prosecutor Alexander Semanas built a case against Turner. Pubic hair found on Lisa's clothing and body matched hair samples taken from Arlene Penn. The hair, which indicated Lisa had been in the Turner-Penn house, also matched in one other respect. Both sets of samples showed evidence of crabs, a parasite.

Penn was a star witness for the prosecution. She described her activities the night of the murder and also, under questioning by Semanas, talked about how she and Turner would view pornographic movies in Oshkosh and have sex afterward.

In his defense, Turner's mother, Dolores, and his ex-wife, Elizabeth, testified that he wasn't capable of murder. But defense attorney Henry Buslee focused his argument on Turner's confession. Turner himself took the stand and claimed Tomaselli and Anderson had coerced him to sign the document and that the words of the confession were not his.

"When does a man reach a point where he says, `All right, I'll sign it,'" Buslee asked the jury.

Although Buslee was unable to convince the jury that the confession was bogus, testimony by Dr. Robert Carlovsky, a pathologist who conducted the autopsy, provided some reprieve for the defendant.

Carlovsky testified that the girl's death was caused by trauma and heart stoppage induced by anal sex.

Buslee swiftly moved for dismissal of the first-degree murder charges. While Turner's actions remained despicable, it appeared the girl's death was not pre-meditated.

Judge Milton Meister, however, wasn't about to let Turner off that easily. Denying the dismissal motion, Meister told Buslee he would instruct the jury on which charges were appropriate.

Turner was convicted of second-degree murder, enticing a child, indecent behavior and sexual perversion. He was sentenced to

36 years in prison.

An appeal to the state Supreme Court claimed there wasn't sufficient evidence to establish that Turner's conduct with the girl was dangerous enough to cause her death. The court refused to grant a new trial, ruling that no miscarriage of justice had occurred.

In the fall of 1992, the Lisa French case again aroused public controversy when Turner was granted parole after serving about 45 percent of his sentence. Many people who recalled the high-profile case petitioned the Parole Board not to grant his release. But the man whom the media had dubbed "the Halloween killer" was released to a halfway house in October, then rented an apartment on Milwaukee's East Side in June 1993.

Turner, who was required to wear an electronic monitoring bracelet as part of the terms of probation, didn't exactly receive a warm welcome from his new neighbors.

"If I lived here and had children, I would move out," one young woman told a reporter. "There's no way I would take that chance."

Today, Lisa French would be of college age. Perhaps she would be attending classes at one of the University of Wisconsin campuses. Maybe she would be married by now with a child of her own. But her life was cut short that Halloween night in 1973 because Gerald Turner maliciously violated her innocent trust.

Chapter 11

Love and death
Madison, 1949

For Sadie and Julius Jackson, it was just a routine trip to the grocery store on that fateful day of July 10, 1949. Julius, a paralyzed World War I veteran, rarely got out of the house. It was just too difficult to move him in and out of the car.

The couple decided to stop at the Norris Court grocery on Madison's East Side after dining at the Park Motor Inn on the Capitol Square for dinner. Julius Jackson recalled the dinner as a particularly memorable evening.

"We enjoyed ourselves so much and we were very, very happy," he said.

And so, Sadie Jackson wanted to stop at the grocery store for a few items after dinner on their way home. Julius Jackson had no objection. He would wait in the car.

While Sadie was inside the store, however, George "Butch" King came up to the Jacksons' parked car.

"Do you mind if I get in?" he asked. Julius recognized King but, before he could reply, King climbed in the back seat.

"He was talking something about my wife running around

with other men and he was all incoherent," Jackson said.

Unaware of King's presence, Sadie Jackson paid for some radishes, a cantaloupe and a head of lettuce, then went outside and crossed the street to where her car was parked. When she got near the car, she saw King get out of the back seat.

"You get out of there!" she said. Still mumbling, King complied, then pushed Sadie against the car.

"You've been running around with too many other men," he said. "I'll teach you a lesson." He pulled a small handgun out of his pocket and fired twice, about eight inches from her chest.

Arthur Fetterhoff was sitting in his car a few feet away. Hearing the shots, he jumped out of his car to come to the aid of Mrs. Jackson while King disappeared in the crowd that had begun to gather.

Sadie Jackson staggered back across the street to grocery store. She fell to her knees and crawled up the front steps. She got to the counter where she had bought her groceries moments before, where Bernard McDermott still stood.

"Shot," was all she could say, clutching the wound oozing blood on her chest. "Shot," she repeated before collapsing to the floor.

To Robert McDermott, Bernard's father and the grocery store owner, the shots from the .25-caliber automatic sounded like firecrackers but his son, Bobby, insisted that McDermott go downstairs to the grocery to investigate. When he got downstairs, he saw several people huddled over Sadie Jackson's body on the floor of the store. She died there, before the ambulance arrived. Outside, a stunned Julius Jackson sat in the car, clutching the bag of groceries and his wife's purse.

It wasn't the first time King had pestered the Jacksons. The previous Saturday night, he approached them while Mrs. Jackson was pushing her husband's wheelchair near Mifflin and Baldwin streeets. Jackson told King to stay away from his wife and wanted to call the police but his wife talked him out of it, saying she was afraid of King because she knew he had a gun.

After the shooting, King, a carpenter, drove back and forth past the murder scene several times before speeding away in his red-panel truck. He abandoned the truck at his daughter's Monona home and fled in his son-in-law's car, a blue 1941 Plymouth sedan. In a daze, he drove for four hours, stopping at the farm of Charles Hull near Stoughton, looking for his daughter. Hull was his daughter's father-in-law. At the farm, King told Hull he had just shot a woman before driving away. Hull immediately notified police. Police found King's truck parked on the Capitol Square, where his daughter and son-in-law had driven it to attend a movie.

Police staked out his home in rural McFarland until they spotted a car that matched the description of the one King was driving. They followed with their police lights and radioed to other units. Police set up a roadblock at Edwards Park, where King was stopped.

"What's this all about?" King said, stepping from the car. He was hand-cuffed and taken to jail.

Before the shooting, pharmacist Clifford Olson noticed King was acting strangely when he visited his Monona Drive pharmacy.

Sadie Jackson

"He was very, very much upset, hysterical and acted just like a maniac," Olson said. "He ran from one end of the store to the other, looking out the front and back windows. He definitely acted rather insane."

Olson had known King for about 16 years. he remembered when King was "a friendly man who you liked to hunt and fish with and liked to be around." That was before he met Sadie Jackson.

King met the pretty, dark-haired waitress a year earlier while he was working on a job near the restaurant where she worked. She had worked at the Park Motor Inn and at the Orin Rime Tavern and Steak House outside the city.

Most people considered Sadie Jackson a dedicated wife who

took good care of her invalid husband and supported him. He had worked as a bartender at the Loraine Hotel but was forced to give it up due to his disability.

Whether Sadie Jackson pursued King or vice versa was an issue at King's trial the following year. But it was clear from her love letters to him that they had a sizzling affair. In the letters, she referred to gifts he had given her such as a sweater and garden produce.

"Never can tell when J.J. (her husband) might take off, so don't think anything of it if I say wrong number," she wrote. "Love you, dearest, much too much."

"I sure did enjoy those two days with you dearest," she wrote in another letter. "Call me Sunday if you get a chance about 2 p.m. I'll be home all day but be sure and ask if I can talk."

When King left town for a carpentry job in Minocqua, she wrote him again: "I'm glad you got on your heavy undies because I know it's cold up there."

"I have you on my mind almost all day," she wrote in still another letter. "This morning, the first song I heard on the radio when I got up was 'My Happiness' and then the one called 'Pretty Eyes.' I'll never forget those songs."

While Sadie Jackson appeared to enjoy the clandestine affair, it took a heavier emotional toll on King. He fell hard for Sadie and was angry when she wanted to break off the affair 11 months after it began.

William King, the grown son of the killer, noticed a dramatic change in his father after the affair began. Sadie Jackson apparently was the first woman Butch King dated after his wife, Molly, died several years earlier.

"He became very thin and sullen and he was not happy," William King said.

King's pharmacist friend, Clifford Olson, also noticed the change.

"He became very snappy, nervous and had a bad temper," Olson said. King also began suffering severe headaches. One time, he took an entire 24-tablet bottle of aspirin to ease the pain. Another time, he asked Olson to give him the same yellow capsules he'd been given by Sadie.

"He said he took 12 or 15 of them at a time and they were the only ones that helped the pains in his head," Olson said.

King's carpentry work also began to suffer. Once known as the best carpenter in Dane County, he built an addition to Clarence Hoyt's Sun Prairie home shortly before the murder and the job was five inches off center.

When Sadie decided to break off the affair, it only aggravated King's problems. He brooded for several weeks before confronting the couple on the sidewalk that Saturday night. The argument only charged his anger. He vowed to himself to punish Sadie somehow. King often packed a small pistol for protection because he carried sums of money from construction jobs in his truck.

On Sunday, the day after the argument, the obsessed, spurned lover spent most of the day driving back and forth in front of the Jacksons' home on East Johnson Street. His thoughts ran to murder-suicide. He would kill Sadie, then turn the gun on himself.

King's murder plot was drawn from a fictional story he had read in a detective magazine called "Bullets Claim Secret Bride." King scrawled a note to his daughter on the magazine page, possibly on Saturday night or Sunday morning: "Leaving to look for her. Hope I have better luck today."

About 5 p.m., he followed the couple to the Park Motor Inn and then to the grocery, where he seized the opportunity to get even.

"She was two-timing me," King later said in a confession to police. "I shot her. I was jealous of her."

King's sensational trial began in late May 1950. At some points, the testimony was so steamy that it offended Judge Alvin Reis.

"There's no necessity for this sort of detail, Mr. Witness," he warned Muriel Thorson, who had spotted King and Sadie in a lover's tryst through the window of King's Blooming Grove home. "Stop that stuff right there."

The trial also featured a touch of controversy when defense attorney Darrell MacIntyre demanded a mistrial because prosecutor Robert Arthur had hired court bailiff John Arnold to help him screen potential witnesses.

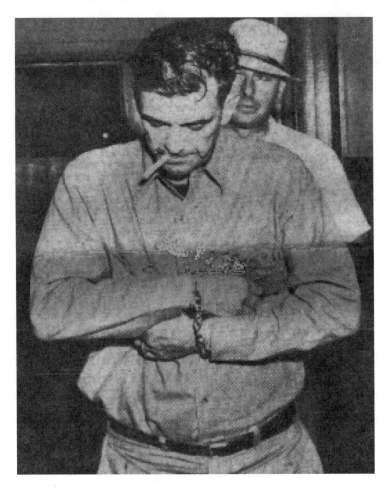

George "Butch" King

"It is reprehensible that the district attorney would use an officer of the court to go out and find a jury that would bring in a conviction," MacIntyre told the judge.

Arthur defended his employment of the bailiff, saying it had been done by other district attorneys.

"Jack is a former sheriff and knows almost everybody," the prosecutor said. "He could do the job quickly and economically and I didn't think there was anything wrong in hiring him."

Arnold had been hired as a special investigator by previous district attorneys but never when he also was serving as court bailiff.

The mistrial motion was denied and the trial went on for nearly four weeks. On a hot Memorial Day afternoon, about 300 people packed the courtroom and a 19-year-old university student fainted from the heat.

On the 19th day, the controversial trial was transferred to the bedside of Dr. Walter Urben, where he lived on the grounds of Mendota State Hospital. Dr. Urben's wife had appeared in court with an affidavit declaring that he was too ill to testify.

But Urben was a key witness because he had conducted a court-ordered mental examination of King the previous fall. The deposition was taken by the judge, bailiff and attorneys without the jury or usual throng of spectators. At one point during the informal proceeding, Dr. Urben stuck his foot out from under the sheet and wriggled it around.

King was convicted of first-degree murder. Due to the mores of the time, Sadie Jackson was viewed as a villain in her own murder. MacIntyre tried to paint a portrait of his client as a good man, misguided by an evil woman who pursued him, then spurned him. Arthur, however, maintained that it was King who chased Jackson, a decent woman devoted to her disabled husband.

The truth probably was somewhere in between. At the time, Sadie Jackson would have been considered a tramp. Today, her actions likely wouldn't be viewed a justification for her murder.

Chapter 12

The capital city killings
Madison, 1968-1982

The university area of Madison, like the city itself, has seemed safe and secure relative to other cities. Until recent years, both the city and the University of Wisconsin campus often exuded a youthful innocence largely unencumbered by violence, poverty and other pressing urban problems. Students often recall their college days of basking in the sun on the Memorial Union terrace or strolling up and down State Street on a warm spring day.

But over a period of fourteen years, a series of bizarre, brutal murders of young women terrorized the peaceful city. What made the slayings more terrifying was that all appeared to be random victims. From 1968 to 1982, seven women were the victims of one or more vicious killers. The victims had striking physical similarities. All were in their late teens or early 20s. All were reasonably attractive, wearing their hair shoulder-length. None of the murders has ever been solved.

The spree began on a spring day of May in 1968, when the body of Christine Rothschild, 18, was found in a clump of bushes outside Sterling Hall, a physics and mathematics building on North Charter Street. Two years later, Sterling Hall would be bombed by anti-war protestors during the throes of Madison's protest era. But on this cool, cloudy day, Rothschild had been viciously stabbed at least a dozen times. The clothed body was found early on a Sunday night, when a male student decided to peek in a window for a friend who worked in the building. Judging from the possible time of death, police theorized the young woman may have been attacked in broad daylight. Besides the stab wounds, they later discovered she also had been strangled.

Christine Rothschild wore her sandy-colored hair long and straight in the style of the time. Students faced upcoming exams and the weather was rainy and muggy, not conducive to being outside. But Christine, who wanted to study journalism, enjoyed early morning walks. Her parents and three sisters lived on Chicago's North Side, where she graduated with honors from Senn High School, finishing with the fourth highest grade-point average in a class of 500 students. Housemothers and other students who lived with her at Ann Emery Hall described her as modest, studious and very attractive. The previous summer, she had worked as a fashion model in Chicago Loop department stores and looked forward that summer to coming home again. Her father was president of a brokerage firm and of a company that sold coin-operated parking lot gates, which he invented during the 1950s.

In an editorial, the Wisconsin State Journal said the murder had "severely shaken" the peace of mind of many Madisonians.

"Many are saying it is inconceivable that such a despicable act could occur here," the newspaper said. "But it did."

While the community was shocked and outraged, police were baffled by the case. A $5,000 reward failed to unearth any significant new clues. A 29-year-old mental patient confessed to the killing but police discounted the confession after viewing his hospital records. Another man suspected of attacking three Carthage College students in Kenosha also was ruled out. During her walk early Sunday, Christine had stopped for breakfast with a man. She ordered a spinach salad. An FBI laboratory report absolved her breakfast companion as a suspect.

As the summer wore on, a doctor at University Hospital

emerged as a possible suspect. Three local lawmen, Madison Detective Charles Lulling, Dane County Sheriff's Sgt. Richard Josephson and Chief Deputy Reynold Abrahams questioned the 43-year-old doctor in New York but his involvement in the case was inconclusive. Lulling and Josephson also worked with Michigan and Iowa campus police, who reported a total of six coeds slain in campus attacks.

Two years later, detectives again were dispatched to the East Coast to interrogate a 27-year-old graduate student who had worked in Sterling Hall at the time of the murder. Like the earlier leads in the case, that one also led nowhere. Police never found the knife, believed to be a double-edged surgical-type blade, used to stab Christine to death.

As the years passed without any new leads, the Rothschild case faded in the community's memory. It appeared to be an aberration, a unique case, unlikely to occur again. Until July 21, 1976. That's when the burned and partially decomposed body of Debra J. Bennett, 20, was found by farm land surveyors in a ditch along Old Sauk Pass Road. The road is about four miles west of Cross Plains, a village in western Dane County. Dr. Billy Baumann, who conducted the autopsy, said the woman probably had been dead about 10 days. The body was identified through dental records and by a fractured collarbone.

Debra Bennett was last seen walking barefoot along Loftsgordon Avenue in Madison, leaving an apartment where she had been evicted. Her toenails were painted and she wore blue jeans, carrying a denim jacket and a brown, shoulder-strap purse. She had rented a room at the Cardinal Hotel but never had the chance to move in. Three weeks after her body was found, the key to her rented room was mysteriously mailed to the hotel.

She was a native of Ridgeway in Iowa County who had lived in Madison about seven months. She was unemployed and her body was found a few days before her 21st birthday. Her death may have contributed to the death of her father, William R. Bennett, who died from an illness a few days after Debra's body was found. A joint funeral for father and daughter was held in Dodgeville.

Like the Rothschild case, police had few leads to solve the murder of Debra Bennett. Two years later, on another summer day, the nude body of another young woman was found in a shallow grave along Woodland Road, just off Highway 12 west of Waunakee. She

apparently had been killed by a blow from a blunt instrument. This time, it took two days to identify the body as Julie Ann Hall.

Julie Ann Hall, 18, grew up in Fennimore. On May 1, 1978, she got a job as a library assistant at the Wisconsin History Society on the university campus. She was the daughter of Donne and Betty Hall who three years earlier had won $300,000 in the Illinois

Julie Ann Hall

state lottery. The couple divorced in late 1977. Julie had seven brothers, one of whom shared an apartment with her in the Park Village Apartments on Madison's South Side. Coroner Clyde Chamberlain said Julie Hall probably was dead about three to five days before her body was found. She was last seen on a Friday night, when she went out drinking with friends. She had been drinking with a male friend at the Main King Tap east of Madison's Capitol Square.

Less than ten months later, another woman named Julie would disappear but the body of Julie Speerschneider, 20, wouldn't be discovered for two years. Julie Speerschneider left the 602 Club, a bar at 602 University Ave., on the night of March 27, 1979, to go to a friend's house. She was wearing blue jeans, boots and a blue-and-gray striped Mexican poncho when she and a male companion hitchhiked along Johnson Street. The driver of a compact, white four-door car had picked up the pair on State Street and left them off at Johnson and Brearly streets. Julie's hitchhiking companion never was identified.

At the time of her disappearance, she worked at the Red Caboose Day Care Center and Tony's Chop Suey Restaurant, where the owner described her as a good employee. Friends and relatives circulated her photograph, offered a $500 reward and consulted a psychic in efforts to locate the missing woman.

In April 1981, Charles Byrd, 16, of Stoughton, was hiking along the Yahara River on a Saturday afternoon when he came across a barely visible skeleton in an out of the way clearing. The remains were those of Julie Speerschneider.

Before Julie Speerschneider's body was found, however, yet another woman would be snatched from Madison's peaceful streets and brutally mur-

Julie Speerschneider

dered. Susan LeMahieu, a 1974 graduate of Madison's East High School, was mildly retarded and physically handicapped. In 1966, when she was age 10, two of her brothers died accidentally when they suffocated in an abandoned refrigerator in the basement of the family's home.

In April 1980, the body of Susan LeMahieu, 24, was found in dense brush of a marsh about 150 feet from a parking lot in the Madison Arboretum. She had been reported missing the prior Dec. 15 from her room at Allen Hall, a residential center for the developmentally disabled.

When Susan LeMahieu's body was found, Shirley Stewart, 17, had been missing for three months. Unlike the other victims, the teenager apparently had no connection with Madison's downtown area. She disappeared Jan. 2, 1980, after finishing her shift at the Dean Clinic, where she worked as a maid.

Shirley Stewart's body was found in July 1981 in a densely wooded area of the town of Westport, north of Madison. By this time, authorities began to see a clear connection between the Bennett, Hall, Speerschneider, LeMahieu and Stewart cases.

"I personally feel there are many similarities," said Deputy Coroner Donald Scullion. "The patterns are wooded areas, off the road aways in a concealed area."

But many of the bodies were severely decomposed by the time they were found, making it difficult even to establish causes of death. The random nature of the killings added to the difficulty in finding what appeared to be a serial killer.

Donna Mraz

Before the murderous spree ended, however, it was to claim one more victim. On July 2, 1982, Donna Mraz, 19, was brutally stabbed a few feet from Camp Randall Stadium on the Madison campus as she walked home from her waitress job at a State Street restaurant. Witnesses heard her screams and rushed to the rescue, only to see her assailant slipping quickly into the shadows.

The case was eerily reminiscent of the Christine Rothschild murder and, like that slaying, offered few clues. Two years afterward, the victim's body was exhumed to compare her teeth to bite marks on a possible suspect in prison. Like many other leads in the seven murders of young Madison women, that lead also evaporated.

In 1984, two years after the Mraz murder, detectives believed they finally had a break in at least some of the killings. In a Texas prison, Henry Lee Lucas was telling investigators that he and side-kick Ottis Toole had murdered more than 100 victims during frequent forays across the country. Detectives David Coachems, Mary Otterson and Herb Hanson were sent to interview Lucas.

The confessed mass killer rocked back and forth in a chair as he told the detectives that, yes, he and Toole had passed through the

Madison area on the way to visit relatives. After nine hours of questioning, the detectives were convinced that Lucas and Toole had killed Julie Ann Hall. After analyzing other evidence presented by Lucas, they also linked him to the murder of Julie Speerschneider.

But then the case against Lucas appeared to unravel as quickly as it had come together. After touring murder sites in several states and describing the brutal crimes to detectives, Lucas suddenly had a change of heart. He had been lying, he said. He and Toole hadn't committed all those murders.

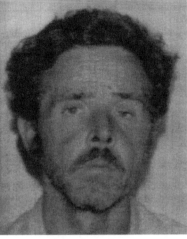

The veteran Madison-area detectives had approached Lucas skeptically and used their best skills

Henry Lee Lucas

trying to find holes in his story. Yet they came away convinced he had committed two of the unsolved crimes. Were they merely the victims of skillful manipulation or was Lucas actually the serial killer stalking young Madison women? The answer may never be known.

Was more than one brutal killer responsible for the deaths of Christine Rothschild, Debra Bennett, Julie Ann Hall, Julie Speerschneider, Susan LeMahieu, Shirley Stewart and Donna Mraz? Was Henry Lee Lucas involved somehow? As the trail on each of these crimes grows colder, the answers to these questions seem ever more elusive.

Chapter 13

A house of cigars

Hancock, 1929

When Elmer Huckins began building his large estate just outside of town in 1929, Hancock residents were intrigued. He
dropped a lot of money at local lumber yards and contractors' offices
for building materials and labor. The Hancock bank reported he
maintained a very healthy account.

The 67-foot by 72-foot, three-story home on 160 acres about
two miles east of town on the west side of Fish Lake would be a gigantic structure few village residents had ever seen. The bathroom
would be done in orchid tile and the dining room was to feature ivory
enamel wainscoting. A glass-enclosed porch with French doors would
encompass the home on three sides. Hand-hewn beams and an enor-
mous fireplace would be the most striking features of the gigantic
living room. Plans included a stable and full-size horse track.

"Just to give an idea of this one building," the Hancock News
reported, "we are told that there are to be 96 doors in it and scores
of vista plate glass windows. Twenty-four telephones will be place on
the premises. Water works and other city conveniences are being
installed."

Besides the horse track, plans also called for a nine-hole golf
course, landscaped gardens and ornamental fences. "No expense is

being spared," the newspaper reported for the permanent home of Elmer and Amelia Huckins.

To most Hancock residents, the tale of Elmer Huckins certainly appeared to be a rags-to-riches story — a story of a very successful American entrepreneur. Just a few years earlier, Huckins operated a small grocery store in the Wood County community of Pittsville and now, here he was, building a huge estate.

The Huckins fortune was amassed with considerable help from his son, George. In his late 30s, George Huckins operated a billiard, cigar and soda business in Cedar Rapids, Iowa. But it wasn't the grocery store or the Iowa business that made the Huckins father and son into millionaires. It was a fradulent investment scheme that bilked investors of thousands of dollars.

Huckins and his son attracted hundreds of investors in what they touted as a can't-miss national cigar business with a promise of 26 percent return on investment, a phenomenal figure, especially for the time. When someone wanted to invest in the Huckins business, he would receive a promissory note that read as follows:

"Received of John Doe the sum of _____ DOLLARS, for which we agree to pay for the same with _____ DOLLARS every forty-five days. First payment due forty-five days from date and other payments every 45 days thereafter as long as we have the use of the money.

"We further agree that this money may be withdrawn or returned at any time by either party giving 60 days notice in writing."

The note would be signed by E.S. (Elmer) Huckins and George S. Huckins.

With the high rate of return and the guarantees in the promissory note, the Huckins family had no problem attracting investors, especially during the late 1920s, an era of fast-and-loose get-rich-quick schemes.

Just as the building of the estate intrigued local residents and the investment terms attracted many people with money, the source of the Huckins fortune caught the attention of state and federal tax investigators.

In early August 1929, a warrant was issued for Elmer Huckins on tax fraud charges. Investigators had discovered that, besides the Hancock estate, Huckins had homes in Chicago and Milwaukee. He also spent the winters in California. A story about Huckins' questionable financial dealings in the Milwaukee Journal caused some investors to become uneasy and they asked for their money back.

Huckins was arrested and he posted the $25,000 bond by putting up his $100,000 home still under construction on Fish Lake. As workers were paving the horse track and putting the finish touches on new tennis courts, he appeared for a hearing before U.S. Commissioner Harry Kellogg.

Prosecutors, however, had moved too soon and it became evident they had only a flimsy case. When the prosecution couldn't produce a single investor who had been defrauded, prosecutor J.T. Koelzor tried valiantly to win a conviction anyway. He brought two witnesses involved in the cigar business who said it was impossible to make money in that business offering such a return on investment. The witnesses also said they had never heard of Huckins, despite his claim to operate a national business in cigars.

"The question of actual fraud and losses does not enter into this case," prosecutor Koelzor said, trying to shore up his weak case. "The purpose of this statute is to prevent fraud."

Several investors testified for the defense, saying they always received their dividend checks on time and had no problems withdrawing funds when they wanted. A star witness was John Niles, who testified that he had invested in the Huckins business and was completely satisfied with the dividends. Niles had retired due to ill health after 27 years as a postal inspector.

"Let them go to the jury," challenged defense attorney Walter Barngrover of Cedar Rapids. "We're not afraid because not a single person has lost a penny during the four years that Huckins has carried on his most successful business."

Kellogg dismissed the charges and admonished the government for bringing such an insubstantial case. He said the prosecution failed to show that Huckins made any false representations to investors.

The Hancock News reported that Kellogg criticized the prosecutors "for not making an exhaustive probe of the financial wizard's business before a warrant for his arrest was issued."

The newspaper fiercely defended its prominent and most wealthy resident:

"Our laborers, businessmen and the community in general have profited from legitimate sources in connection with the remarkable project at Fish Lake and at a time when business was at a low ebb throughout this region," the newspaper stated. "Mr. Huckins has brought money into this community instead of taking it away. He has been a heavy depositor in our bank and never a borrower there. We have heard of no unpaid bills against him anywhere."

Was the Huckins business legitimate? Could he really reward investors with a 26 percent rate of return and make a fortune at the same time? It didn't seem possible and it wasn't. Despite the dismissal by Kellogg, authorities weren't about to give up.

The legal struggles didn't slow down the efforts by Elmer and George Huckins to woo investors. In fact, those efforts seemed only to intensify.

Emil Levson, a creamery owner in Springville, Iowa, later told of meeting George Huckins at his Cedar Rapids cigar store in late October 1929, about a month after the court hearing in Milwaukee.

Huckins told Levson that his father had a business in cigars with a profit margin of 52 percent; that big manufacturers had to buy tobacco three or four years in advance and that there was always a surplus; and that his father bought this stock of cigars and sold them as seconds. All shipments were made from factory to retailer in large lots eight times a year, Huckins said.

Levson asked George Huckins how much the business earned each year.

"Thirty million dollars," Huckins replied. "And outside investors put up only two percent of the money. My father and I put up the balance."

Levson thought a moment. "But how can your father do such a great business without a lot of employees?"

George smiled. "It's simple. All we need are three girls in the Chicago office and actually one could do all the work."

"How can you make such huge profits?"

"We don't have to employ salesmen, advertise or maintain a large warehouse."

The explanation seemed logical to Levson. Huckins suggested to Levson that he invest about $5,000. When Levson hesitated, Huckins upped the ante. He offered a 52 percent return on investment.

"If you get your friends to invest, you can give them 26 percent and keep 26 percent. How about it?"

It sounded good to Levson but he didn't have $5,000. He invested $300 instead.

The deal offered to Levson and other investors also sounded too good to investigators, who remained hot on the trail of Elmer and George Huckins. As the probe into the Huckins family fortune deepened, it became clear that the entire cigar-buying scheme was nothing but a scam.

Early in 1930, Elmer and George Huckins were indicted on fraud charges by a grand jury in Linn County, Iowa. The district attorney and sheriff of that county were dispatched to Wisconsin to seek extradition of Elmer Huckins from Gov. Walter Kohler. After some deliberation, the governor agreed. But local authorities intervened and Huckins won the right to a *habeas corpus* hearing before Wautoma Court Commissioner Charles Taylor to determine whether he was being held illegally. When Taylor set bond at $5,000, Huckins quickly posted the money and returned to his home on Fish Lake.

At the same time, George Huckins, who had been held on $10,000 bond, was admitted to a Cedar Rapids hospital for treatment of a drug-related illness.

By February 1930, the supposed Huckins fortune was showing serious cracks. Liens totaling over $13,000 were filed against the estate by architect Frank Drolshagen of Milwaukee, landscaper Carl Gerlach of Milwaukee and the Louis Hoffman Co., a furnace installer. A new Cadillac bought by Huckins a few months earlier was sold at auction to offset an unpaid balance of $3,400 on the car.

Another creditor, E.J. Courtney, took his case to the newspaper. Courtney was the caretaker at the Huckins estate and worried about collecting $1,000 in back wages. Courtney's tale, however, shed little light on Huckins' financial activities and only seemed to raise more questions.

"Some weeks ago, I had a showdown with Huckins about my salary," Courtney told the Milwaukee Journal. "I told him that I didn't believe that he had any business and he said he would show me.

"He handed me something that he said was a contract and a note. It was signed 'A. Andrews' and was for $2.6 million, and I read an agreement to pay Huckins $17,600 every 45 days. He didn't let me examine the contract long -- I just had a glance at it, so I don't know much of what it is about."

"Neither Huckins nor his son, George, is a smart man but the elder Huckins has a great personality. He knows how to handle strangers. He doesn't give them too much bunk, just enough to impress them."

Courtney said he had heard Huckins had a reserve fund of $52 million in New York. "But I am willing to take my pay and let the $52 million go."

In March 1930, an Iowa jury deliberated 25 hours before finding George Huckins guilty of obtaining money under false pretenses. On the same day, Elmer Huckins was turned over to Iowa authorities for extradition. This time, Elmer Huckins couldn't pay the $22,000 bail and he was placed in a Cedar Rapids jail cell.

After another trial in Milwaukee, the elder Huckins was convicted on Oct. 3, 1930. In July 1931, Elmer and George Huckins were indicted by a federal grand jury in connection with the elaborate investment scheme. Also indicted were Elmer's wife, Amelia; Martha Kiley, a relative; and John Niles. Niles, the former postal clerk who helped persuade the judge to dismiss the earlier charges against the Huckins', apparently had helped woo other investors.

The strain of the legal battles and the fall from grace apparently was too much for George. On a Sunday morning in 1932, a jailer brought breakfast to his cell and found him dead. He was 42 and looking forward to his release on bond within a few weeks. An autopsy found that George Huckins died of heart disease. The pressure also apparently got to John Niles, aggravating his illness. He died a month before George Huckins.

In early 1933, Elmer Huckins was sentenced to 15 years in Fort Leavenworth penitentiary and fined $10,000. Amelia Huckins, remained on the run but charges against her were dropped by Judge F.A. Geiger. In 1938, Elmer Huckins died in a prison hospital at age 72.

Before Elmer's death, the Huckins estate was acquired by Ben Baker, a Hancock lumberman. It remained vacant for nearly a decade before it was bought on July 23, 1945, by Leo Grassman, who operated a Madison riding academy. The Shangri La, a summer camp for girls, opened the following year. Later, the estate changed hands again, becoming the Camp St. Michaels, a summer camp for boys.

The Huckins' national cigar business certainly seemed more fantasy than reality, although there is no question that the father and son duo collected tens of thousands in hard cash. Early investors received their dividends when the two men rolled over the money put up by later investors. The later investors and many tradesmen who worked on the huge estate simply lost their money.

But for a few short months, the luxurious furnishings and oriental rugs that cost $25,000 apiece created a sense of awe at the opulence for many Hancock residents, just before the nation was plunged into the Great Depression.

Chapter 14

Living with a cat

Wautoma, 1967

James "Butch" McBrair had been drinking early on March 5, 1967, when he reached through a plastic window to unlock the back door of a cottage on Fish Lake near Wautoma. It was a cottage where, until their separation, he had lived with his wife, Carol, and their two daughters.

In high school, Butch had starred in basketball in high school but life seemed to go sour ever since. McBrair would say later that through his foggy brain he seemed to hear voices — talking or yelling in duplicate or triplicate. As he entered the kitchen, he leaned his .22-caliber semi-automatic rifle against the wall next to the door. Someone said something about calling the sheriff. McBrair went back outside and yanked out the phone wires.

"Does he have a gun?" McBrair recalled hearing someone say through the blur. He picked up the gun and turned around, seeing a figure in a dark jacket coming at him. "Get the hell out of here, McBrair!" a voice said.

He lifted the gun and fired two or three times, lighting up the kichen with the flash. He ran into the house toward the girls' playroom, passing a woman crouched in a doorway. McBrair ran into a bedroom and nearly toppled into a bed, then turned and ran back to the living room. He heard a voice coming from the kitchen and saw someone coming toward him out of the corner of his eye. He turned and fired several times but the shots didn't seem to slow down the man, who went to the phone. Somehow, according to McBrair's account, his estranged wife, Carol, grabbed the gun and the struggle moved outside. Wading through the deep snow and slipping on ice, McBrair tried to get the gun away from her but she tried to bite his hand. He grabbed a garbage can lid and tried to hit her, then noticed an axe lying at his feet.

"Oh, my God, no!" Carol McBrair cried as her husband picked up the axe. She dropped the gun. McBrair picked up the gun and headed back toward the cottage with his wife following. She shouted that he needed help. She grabbed the gun again and McBrair fired several times, fatally wounding his wife at close range. She dropped to her knees and told him to kill her.

"Something rang through my head about dad always saying never leave anything suffer," McBrair would say later. "It seemed like I was hunting. They didn't seem like people to me."

He reloaded the gun and went back to the cottage to finish off all the victims. While he was shooting, McBrair felt something tugging at his pants leg. It was his youngest daughter, Kathy, 5.

"Please don't shoot anymore, Daddy," she pleaded. "We have blood on us." McBrair put the two girls in bed with their slain babysitter and left the cottage.

About 4 a.m., McBrair's father, James Sr., heard a noise downstairs. "Is that you, Butch?" he asked, but there was no answer. The elder McBrair found his soon in the living room, looking disoriented.

"I shot Marge, Marve, Carol and someone else," McBrair told his dad. "You better call the sheriff."

Besides his wife, McBrair had brutally murdered Marve Behr, his father-in-law; Barbara Behr, his 15-year-old sister-in-law; and Sheryl Oleson, the babysitter. He mistakenly thought one of the victims was Marge Behr, his mother-in-law.

About 5:30 a.m., Waushara County Sheriff Virgil "Buck" Batterman picked up Deputy Edward Oligney at home.

"We have a bad one," the tight-lipped sheriff told him.

About 15 minutes later, the lawmen approached the cottage. The lights were on and two cars were parked in the driveway. The outside light was on, a door was ajar and, as Oligney later described it, "there was a striking silence about the place." In the kitchen, he noticed a Sumari-type sword lying on the floor.

"Hey!" Batterman shouted.

"Anybody home?" Oligney yelled.

Batterman reached the bedroom and the light from his flashlight swept across the floor. "Oh, my God!" he said. Two bodies were on the floor and three more were in the bed. Both of the people on the floor were dead. Oligney noticed the two children in bed were still breathing, lying with their faces to the wall. Batterman left to recruit a local newspaper photographer to take pictures of the scene and Oligney found the body of Marve Behr in the living room. Oligney took the two girls home. The next morning, Mrs. Oligney fixed breakfast for the girls.

"My mommy won't mind if we stay here," Kristie said. "My daddy shot my mommy and she's never coming back." Later, Kristie observed that "grandpa was the worst because he had more blood on him."

For James McBrair, the murders marked the lowest point of his life. Now 27, he had been a handsome lad, growing up on a 400-acre farm near Plainfield, made famous by the grave-robbing, murders and crafting of human remains of Ed Gein a few years earlier. At Tri-County High School, the tall, blond, young McBrair was a star athlete in basketball and football. He was prom king, class vice president and a B student. In his junior year, he played a lead role in the school play. To those who knew him, it seemed incredible that a young man held in such high esteem could commit such a gruesome crime.

Many small-town athletes seem to reach their peak in high school. Some leave for college and find they can't handle the lack of recognition in a larger city. They often return home in an effort to recapture those years of glory. For McBrair, his world began to crumble before he graduated. During his senior year, he married Barbara Cummings in a shotgun marriage. The couple had three children before they separated. Then, McBrair met the beautiful Carol Behr.

Carol, who also had three children by a previous marriage, moved in with McBrair at the family farm near Plainfield. But McBrair's father finally asked them to leave after he became upset that Carol seemed to be coming and going at all hours of the night. The couple married and moved to Milwaukee, later moving back to Waushara County and renting the cottage on Fish Lake.

As McBrair's trial loomed, he worked with a court-appointed attorney, Jon Wilcox, to prepare his defense. A crucial part of the defense was building a case against the victim, his wife, Carol. McBrair and his lawyer hoped to plant the idea in the jury's mind that she got what she deserved.

"Living with Carol was like living with a cat," McBrair said. "She could change from one mood to another faster than anyone I ever knew. She could change from a purr to a snarling fighter at the drop of a hat."

McBrair recalled the night he met Carol. Both had been drinking at a local watering hole. When Carol went to the bathroom, a male friend with them elbowed McBrair and winked.

"You've got it made tonight, Butch," he said. "Get one of the Behr girls drunk and you've got a sure sack job."

During the first part of the trial, the state had no trouble proving that McBrair committed the murders. Then the trial went into a second phase as the jury was asked to decide whether McBrair suffered from a mental disease at the time of the killings. Before the trail, he had been examined by several psychiatrists.

In the first blow to the state's case, Dr. E.F. Schubert, superintendent at Central State Hospital, testified that McBrair was insane and that testimony was corroborated by a defense psychiatrist.

Then McBrair himself took the stand. His straight-forward testimony of his early life, two failed marriages and the killings clearly impressed the judge, Robert Gohlmar.

"My own impression of the defendant was a sincere, remorseful young man who was caught in an emotional trap from which he could escape no other way," Gohlmar later wrote of the case in his book, *Tales of a Country Judge*. "His crimes horrified me, but I felt an instinctive liking for this confused and unhappy man."

Jurors also showed sympathy for the young man, apparently agreeing somewhat with the defense's contention that McBrair was wronged and driven to murder by his promiscuous wife. In the end, however, they found him sane and guilty of murder.

It's significant that the case reflected social attitudes of the time. McBrair's defense of claiming his wife's promiscuity had caused his insanity wouldn't fly today, in an era where women are judged more equally and divorce is more common. Clearly, jurors today would question why McBrair just didn't divorce his wife if he was upset about her conduct.

In prison, McBrair accepted his punishment and refused to allow his attorneys to appeal to the state Supreme Court. He pursued a college degree and, unlike Douglas Dean, his charm and efforts apparently impressed parole officials. In a case with some similarities to McBrair, Dean murdered his mother and three members of his girlfriend's family in 1970.

But Dean, who earned a doctorate in psychology and argued he had been reformed by the prison system, remains imprisoned while McBrair was paroled after serving 14 years. Members of a state pardon board called McBrair "the epitome of the rehabilitative process" and McBrair's parole efforts also were supported by University of Wisconsin-Madison Dean Mary Rouse, who came to know McBrair when he was imprisoned at Oak Hill Correctional Institution in Oregon and took courses at the university.

Today, McBrair has remarried and lives quietly in northern Wisconsin near the upper Michigan border. But the suffering hasn't ended for all of his victims. His daughter, Kathy, who witnessed the brutal crimes a quarter century ago is working on a book about the case. While she supported her father's clemency efforts, now she feels cheated of her mother's companionship by her father's awful deed.

Chapter 15

A stick and a haystack
Portage, 1922

His sister's autumn romance didn't set well with Hartwell Farwell. Why couldn't she leave well enough alone?

Farwell and his sister, Alice, had lived together on the Dane County farm in the town of Vienna for decades. They both owned the farm equally. He couldn't understand why a woman in her 50s suddenly would want a beau.

Besides that, Farwell had a particular dislike for Theophil Hosten, the man Alice had decided to date. Hosten had worked on the Farwell farm for nine years and left only after frequent arguments with Farwell, his boss. Hosten, who called Alice "my girl," had told his friends that Alice was tired of living on the family farm and wanted to leave. She and Hosten planned to buy a chicken farm of their own.

Farwell had disdain for all his workers and that one would have the audacity to begin dating his sister particularly infuriated him. What if Hosten married his sister and moved in with them? Would he then have equal rights to the farm?

These thoughts no doubt were running through his head one evening in early January 1922 when Hosten stopped by the farm to see Alice. Several versions of the events that followed were offered by Farwell and his sister but there's no question that Hosten ended up with two fatal .32-caliber bullet wounds in his head.

A few days later, Dr. Charles Curtiss of Portage was driving by a deserted marsh about three miles from Portage when he noticed a burning haystack. When he stopped to take a closer look, he noticed a section of hay fall way to reveal some kind of object in the stack. Curtiss managed to drag a body from the flames.

The body appeared almost impossible to identify. Part of the face was burned away and one leg had been consumed by flames. Although the body was charred, investigators could tell the victim hadn't died in the fire. He was killed by a bullet that passed through his right eye into his head. Another bullet wound was found in a cheek.

He was wearing a sheepskin coat and khaki shirt, indicating he may have been a soldier. The body had been placed in gunny sacks.

The Wisconsin State Journal called the case "the most baffling mystery in that section of the state." But authorities wouldn't be baffled very long.

A key with the inscription "E.1.6." matched a padlock on a small garage in the town of Windsor owned by Hosten, who by this time had been reported missing.

After authorities questioned acquaintances of Hosten and his two roommates, it wasn't difficult to pinpoint a suspect. When they found tire tracks in the snow matching the tires on Farwell's car, it clinched the case and they brought Farwell in for questioning.

He readily confessed, admitting that he shot Hosten about 7 p.m. or 8 p.m. on Jan. 10. He left him in a wooded area across the road for a couple hours, then carried the body to his barn. The next night, he moved the body again to a tobacco shed. On Jan. 12, Farwell loaded the body into his car, intending to dump it somewhere in Madison. Instead, he headed in the other direction. When he spotted the haystack, he decided that was as good a place as any to get rid of Hosten once and for all. Farwell even admitted he had Hosten's watch and chain in his room. A spot of blood was found near the doorway of Farwell's hog barn and marks on the floor indicated something had been dragged across there.

Farwell spent his 50th birthday confined in the Dane County Jail and Sheriff William McCormick was congratulated on a quick resolution of the case.

For a short time, authorities thought Farwell might have had an accomplice. A pair of youths had been skating on a pond near Poynette. They claimed to have seen Farwell and another man drive up. They said Farwell got out of his car and peered through a hole in the ice, perhaps looking for a place to dump the body. The story proved to be mere gossip.

The confession might have cleared the case easily but Farwell added a bombshell. He said he had shot Hosten in self-defense. He said he heard a noise outside and went out to investigate. He saw Hosten move toward him carrying a stick,

Hartwell Farwell

making it look like he had a gun. Hosten fired three times, missing on the first shot.

Meanwhile, Alice Farwell offered several versions of what occurred that night to police.

"I don't know why I said no before (but) I did see Phil," she said. "I was washing dishes when I heard a tap on the window. It was about 7 or 7:30. I looked out but saw nothing and then went into the front room without seeing anything.

"I went back and washed the dishes. Then I took the dish water and went out through the kitchen door to throw it out. I saw Phil just around the corner. I went on toward him and told him to go away because my brother was here. He did not embrace me and we did not touch either.

"My brother was upstairs. I heard the door on the opposite side of the house open and I went back in the way I had come. I didn't hear any shots fired. I know that my brother saw Phil had come but don't know what happened.

"I did tell the sheriff that I didn't remember a time when five shots were fired at Phil as he passed the house. But now I'll admit I heard the shots at that time. Of course, I can't say for sure that it was my brother."

Farwell's self-defense ploy didn't hold up very long because, at his preliminary hearing, Alice offered a different version. She said she had seen her boyfriend running away from her brother just before he was shot. Farwell was charged with first-degree murder.

The stick that looked like a shotgun was explained by Joe "Belgian Joe" Carlier, a friend of Hosten.

"Phil had a homemade cane, (made) out from some brush, that he always carried when he went to see his girl," Carlier said. "There was a bad dog along the way and it was for this reason that he carried the stick that night, the same as he always did."

By the time of the trial, Farwell was considering an insanity plea. He didn't fare well in jail and tottered into court, almost like he had trouble walking. He was suffering from lumbago, stomach trouble and a general breakdown.

Alice and her brother had tried to coordinate their stories. But District Attorney Ted Lewis had a more convincing version: He said Farwell had gone upstairs to fill an oil lamp. He looked out in the front yard and saw his sister with Hosten. He walked to a dresser, pulled out a loaded revolver and walked outside to shoot Hosten. After dragging the body to the woods, he milked the cows, apparently undisturbed by what had just occurred.

When Alice took the stand, she said Hosten had tapped on the window and motioned for her to join him outside. She said she warned Hosten that her brother was angry and he should leave, then went back inside and resumed her chores. Refuting her earlier testimony, she said she didn't see Hosten running away or the actual shooting.

Farwell continued to maintain that the shooting was in self-defense. But the stick Hosten was carrying had mysteriously disappeared. Farwell said he had cut it up because it was "strange" and he didn't want it around.

The prosecutor noted another inconsistency in Farwell's testimony. Farwell said he could see the eyes of his victim yet he couldn't distinguish a stick from a gun.

Alice, who had tried her best to help save her brother, once again came forward with damaging testimony. She told the court how Farwell once had chased Hosten with a pitchfork. In that incident, Hosten had returned and threatened Farwell with a shotgun.

The jury deliberated for 48 hours before finding Farwell guilty of the murder of Theophil Hosten. Farwell, a prominent farmer and trustee of the Windsor Congregational Church, was sentenced to seven years in prison.

Hartwell Farwell came by his protective attitude toward his sister naturally. His father, James, had discouraged Alice and her sisters from marrying. John Butler, another hired hand, earlier had set a date with Alice to get married but James Farwell intervened.

"I've got money enough to support my daughters and they don't need to marry for support," he told Butler. One of Alice's sisters married Ole Anderson despite her father's opposition. She wasn't allowed to attend James Farwell's funeral when he died a decade before the Hosten murder.

The murder didn't dampen Alice's romantic ardor nor did it cure her brother's jealousy. She married Harry G. Phillips but they were divorced in 1932. Her brother didn't shoot Phillips but he didn't like him any more than Hosten.

Before the divorce, Alice and Phillips fought in court three times, once over a bay horse that Phillips said was his. Phillips said that her brother Hartwell, then known as the "gray deacon of the township of Vienna" had put her up to it. Phillips, who acted as his own attorney, accused Hartwell of stealing produce from his farm and selling it but the judge said Hartwell had a right to visit the Phillips farm if his sister invited him.

Chapter 16

Unless he's a soldier

Tomah, 1942

S omething bothered Anne Baun about the idea of her daughter driving across Wisconsin from Kenosha to Sparta.

"Why don't you take the train?" she suggested. "I just don't like it, Dorothy."

"Oh, mother, don't worry," Dorothy Baun replied. "I'll be riding with Neil."

"I still don't like it — the two of you girls alone out on the highway. But I guess there's no talking you out of it. Well then, if you must go, just don't you go picking up any hitchhikers."

"We won't," Dorothy promised. "Unless he's a soldier!"

How could Anne Baun argue with that? It was early September 1942, after all, and the nation had been at war with Japan and Germany for less than 10 months. Giving a solider a ride seemed like a patriotic thing to do.

The flash of independence shown by Dorothy Baun toward her mother wasn't out of character for the times. The war seemed to enhance the independence of many women, making it acceptable to stay single and pursue careers. Women were expected to contribute to the war effort by filling the jobs left behind by men who had gone to war. Afterward, most women would go back to their roles as house-wives until the late 1960s and early 1970s when the modern feminist movement took hold.

Dorothy Baun and her friend, Neil Pietrangeli, were rather plain-looking women in their early 30s. Both held state jobs as social workers. Dorothy had worked less than a month as a case worker for the State Parole Board at Eau Claire. Neil had been a case worker for two years at the State School for Dependent Children in Sparta.

Neil Pietrangeli

Dorothy had graduated six years earlier from Stout Institute (now the UW-Stout) in Menomonie. Her new job involved monitoring women on probation or recently paroled from Tacycheedah State Prison. Neil, a graduate of Lake Forest College who did postgraduate work at the University of Chicago, was responsible for supervising the placement of children in private homes from the school in Sparta.

The two women first met in Kenosha County, where Dorothy had been employed by the county probation department and Neil was a welfare worker. That weekend in early September, the women decided to visit some of their old haunts. Both were scheduled to return to work on Tuesday and Dorothy planned to drive with her friend to Sparta, then take a bus to Eau Claire.

They left Kenosha about 5 p.m. in Neil's 1941 light-green Oldsmobile coupe. About 7 p.m., they stopped in Sauk City and bought 10 gallons of gasoline. They never made it to Sparta and L.H.

Schroeder, the gas station attendant, apparently was the last person to see the two women alive.

Alick Chambers was driving his milk truck along Highway C near Tomah about 7 a.m. the next morning. It seemed like a routine fall morning as he made his regular milk pick-ups when he suddenly spotted something lying along the side of the road. At first he thought it might be a dead animal, perhaps a deer. But when he looked closer, Chambers saw it was a badly wounded nude woman. He braked his truck and pulled over, then ran back to where the woman lay to see if he could help.

Dorothy Baun

"My friend is in the bushes there," Dorothy Baun said as Chambers helped the dying woman into his truck. "They hit us and robbed us. There is another girl up there in the woods hurt worse than I cam."

She was covered with mud and bleeding severely from multiple bullet wounds. Chambers raced to the nearest doctor for help but it was too late. Dorothy Baun died en route.

Neil Pietrangeli was found minutes later. She had clung to life for about a hour after she was shot before she also succumbed to her gunshot wounds. She had been shot with a large-caliber revolver in the abdomen, side and shoulder. Dorothy Baun had been shot seven times in the back.

Before the shooting, the assailant forced the women to disrobe and raped them, although Neil still wore a brassiere when she was found. Their car, purses and clothes were missing but their watches, jewelry, shoes and stockings were found nearby. Police theorized the assailant carried the women to the thicket where Pietrangeli was found. After raping the women, he shot each of them several times. Dorothy Baun apparently crawled out of the bushes to the roadside seeking help.

Less than an hour after Chambers happened on the murder scene, Pvt. Edward Helgeson a Chippewa Falls soldier on furlough from a New Jersey Army camp was hitchhiking near Tomah when a light-green Oldsmobile stopped to pick him up. When the hitchhiker threw his duffel bag into the trunk, he noticed women's clothing inside. The driver, also a solider in uniform, had been drinking heavily, the hitchhiker later told authorities, and bragged he had "stolen the car from two girls."

The biggest clue, however, was a $10 paycheck from the Kenosha welfare department endorsed by Dorothy Baun and cashed by a soldier at a Tomah gas station on Monday night — minutes after the two women were left for dead.

As gas station attendent Ralph Hilgen filled the tank of the Oldsmobile, the soldier told him he was coming from an Army camp in the South to visit his sweetheart. He guzzled a bottle of pop and those who saw him, including Hilgen, later described the man's demeanor as calm and deliberate.

"We'll have the murderer before night," vowed Monroe County Sheriff Hallet T. Jenkins. But it wouldn't be that easy.

Another $25 check made out to Neil Pietrangeli was cashed later Tuesday at a bank in Le Seuer, Minn. Bank cashier J.D. Peterson said the man who presented the check wore an Army uniform and used the name of Robert Bailey.

"When I asked him about signing her name to the check, he told me the signature was authorized in a Sparta, Wis. bank," Peterson later told authorities.

He accepted the check without further question , writing the man's Army serial number on the back. The check was forwarded for collection to a bank clearing house in Chicago.

Another report led authorities in the opposite direction. A bundle of women's clothing, including two girdles, lingerie, several pairs of stockings, gloves, a striped pink gown and a polka-dotted dress were found near Gary, Ind. But the clothing turned into a false lead when relatives of the two slain women were unable to identify it as owned by the victims.

As suscipions focused on a military man, Monroe County District Attorney Leo Goodman met with officials at nearby Camp McCoy and Camp Williams. A list of soliders on leave at the time of the slayings was compiled and photographs were gathered of all soldiers AWOL (absent without official leave). A tip prompted authorities to check for suspects at the Madison Air Forces Technical School. These efforts, however, also failed to locate the killer.

In Santa Clara, Calif., Robert Taylor Bailey arrived a few days later at the home of Cyril Simmeon. Bailey was accompanied by a pair of 16-year-old girls he had picked up in Sioux City, Iowa. One of the girls was a niece of Mrs. Simmeon.

Simmeon thought it was mighty suspicious that Bailey was trying to paint the whitewalls on the 1941 Oldsmobile he was driving. Simmeon contacted police, who connected Bailey's name with the person who had endorsed the check in Minnesota. Strangely, he had used his real name. When detectives questioned him, it wasn't for them difficult to persuade Bailey to confess. Not only did investigators find the Oldsmobile, but they also found many belongings of the two women in Bailey's possesion. In short, they had him cold.

"I am the man wanted for the Wisconsin murders," he said calmly.

In fact, Bailey offered four separate confessions, each differing significantly in the details. First, he said his accomplice was a man named Joe Cortez, who forced the women off the highway and actually raped them. Then, he claimed the accomplice was Manuel Smith. Bailey said Smith shot the women "when they raised too much hell." Bailey claimed he later shot Smith and dumped his body in the St. Croix River.

Another confession named his accomplice as Jesse Fletcher, with whom Bailey had escaped a year earlier from a Mississippi reformatory. Later, Bailey said he named Fletcher to get even for a grudge he carried against him.

Despite the mystery surrounding Bailey's possible accomplice, some facts were clear: Bailey had deserted his Army post at Fort Bragg, stealing a .45-caliber revolver. He fled to Ohio, then Chicago, hitch-hiking to Madison on Sept. 7. About 75 miles from Madison along Highway 12, he hitched a ride with Dorothy Baun and Neil Pietrangeli.

Bailey forced the two women to drive down a rural road. He made them disrobe and go into the woods, where he finally admitted raping "the smaller one" (Pietrangeli).

He fled into Minnesota where, ironically, he was taken into custody on a minor charge by Minneapolis police but released after telling the officers he was on the way to visit his mother in Tacoma, Wash. The officers dropped him off at the train station but Bailey instead drove the Oldsmobile to Sioux City, where he met the two girls.

He waived extradtion back to Wisconsin, pleaded guilty to the murder of Neil Pietrangeli and, in late September, Bailey was sentenced to life in prison. He wasn't charged with the murder of Dorothy Baun, possibly so he could be charged with that murder if, despite the confession, he somehow got off the first murder charge.

Bailey was 20 years old at the time of the murders yet already a hardened criminal. At age 11, he was sent to reform school for burglary. Two years later, he was back in reform school on another felony charge.

When he was arrested for the Baun-Pietrangeli murders, Bailey's father wrote a letter to Monroe County Sheriff Jenkins. The elder Bailey said he was glad his son was arrested so he couldn't cause any more trouble.

Chapter 17

Slaughter of a family
Athens, 1987

Athens, namesake of the ancient Greek city of learning and en-
lightenment, is a sleepy, rural town of less than 1,000 residents
in north central Wisconsin. The village lies about six miles north of
Highway 29, the main artery between Wausau and Chippewa Falls.

In a dilapidated farmhouse on a dirt road west of Athens, four
bodies were found in early July 1987. Each of the victims was shot
twice in the head with a small-caliber weapon.

Kenneth Kunz lived in a travel trailer next to the farmhouse.
When he came over to the main house after the Fourth of July, Kunz
found the bodies of his Uncle Clarence, 76, his aunts Marie, 72, and
Irene, 82, and his brother, Randy, 30. Missing was Kunz' mother,
Helen, 70. She was last seen attending a Fourth of July fireworks dis-
play with Randy.

Discovery of the slain Kunz family not only became one of
Wisconsin's most perplexing murder mysteries. It also provided a
glimpse into the bizarre relationships of an isolated and unusual farm
family.

Believing the missing woman to be the key to the case, Marathon County Sheriff Leroy Schillinger quickly circulated a three-year-

old photograph of Helen Kunz. The faded photograph showed an elderly woman in a babushka and winter coat. Her eyes were closed and her head cocked to one side while her mouth curled upward in what could be a half-smile.

Could Helen Kunz have played a role in the murders? Was she the cold-blooded executioner who methodically put her family to death? Schillinger wasn't sure but the sheriff believed finding Helen would lead to answers to these questions. He began the search by ordering his deputies to comb the swampy woodlands behind the farmhouse.

Helen Kunz stood 5 feet 3 inches tall and weighed 113 pounds. At the fireworks display, she wore a white blouse with a large floral print, slacks and sneakers.

The family farmhouse had no indoor plumbing and cooking was done on a woodstove. But the family had a microwave oven, a videotape recorder and a television set covered in plastic. One investigator remarked the plastic covering almost made it appear the family viewed the television set as sacred. Rooms were cluttered with stacks of newspapers, piles of magazines, garbage and other items in paper

The Kunz farm, scene of the family slaughter.

bags. Investigators used an end-loader to move a four-foot stack of boxes, old newspapers and magazines from the attic. Detectives wearing rubber gloves sorted through the debris.

Hidden in the messy house, however, investigators found something far more valuable than old newspapers and magazines. They found cash, lots of it, all over the house. More than $20,000 was recovered but authorities refused to rule out robbery as a motive in the killings.

"There was no way of knowing if twice that amount was taken," said District Attorney Rand Krueger.

Early on, investigators also discovered a strange twist to the case that went back several decades. In 1933, when Helen Kunz was 15, a neighbor named Frank Gumz was convicted of raping her in the hayloft. During the trial, exactly 54 years before the murders, Helen testified that she became pregnant as a result of the rape and had a son named Kenneth. In his defense, Gumz' lawyer tried to prove the boy was fathered by Helen's brother, Clarence, instead.

Gumz was sentenced to 18 months at Waupun Correctional Institution and later transferred to Central State Hospital for the Insane. He died in a car accident in 1936. Years later, Kenneth Kunz would claim that his real father was Clarence Kunz, his uncle.

After the bodies were found, Schillinger told reporters he was investigating continuing reports of incestuous relationships within the family. He suggested that Kenneth Kunz or his missing mother could be suspects.

"It has many, many twists," he said.

By the time of the murders, the Kunz family didn't farm the land themselves anymore. Clarence Kunz had grown oats and hay on the 108-acre tract until his health gave out and he wound up renting the land to neighbors. Neighbors saw little of the reclusive family. They watched 81-year-old Irene split wood for the stove and carry it inside. The elderly sisters tended a vegetable garden and Randy routinely drove his mother into town, where she paid bills, shopped for groceries, did her laundry and tended to other family business.

Helen Kunz also complained about the "dirty movies" other family members liked to watch on the videotape machine. Gale

Weiler, who ran Wieler's Hardware Hank in Athens, recalled Helen's comments when she once accompanied Kenneth to town to buy some ammunition. The movies, coupled with the allegations of incest, helped create an atmosphere of sexual intrigue surrounding the family and the killings. Did Helen kill her family over the movies and then disappear? Were the family members killed in some kind of lover's quarrel or settle an old score? Schillinger believed he wouldn't find out until Helen herself was found.

"You find me Helen, and I'll probably tell you what happened," he told reporters.

He hoped, of course, that Helen would be found alive, that she had been taken hostage or escaped after playing a role in the murders. Although Kenneth was cooperative with authorities, he couldn't provide answers about the family's violent demise and the case continued to puzzle investigators. Air and ground searches of the farm failed to turn up a body, a weapon or a single clue.

Through the summer and early fall, the sheriff received numerous reports that Helen had been sighted. None of the reports checked out. Schillinger asked deer hunters to help in the search. Meanwhile, residents of the German-Polish village of Athens were terrified by the crime. Before the murders, the 988 residents hadn't been concerned about locking their doors. That changed dramatically after the grisly discovery on the Kunz farm.

By January 1988, investigators had identified several suspects. They began a methodical examination of guns owned by area residents. When .22-caliber shell casings were found in a room during a search of a Medford home, Chris Jacobs III became the strongest suspect. Two rifles, ammunition and a car were among the items seized at the 93-acre Jacobs farm.

An analysis of the shell casings by the Wisconsin Crime Laboratory found they matched casings found at the Kunz farm. But it would be nine months before investigators built a case they felt was strong enough to arrest Jacobs. He was questioned, charged with being party to the crime of murder and released.

Word that people with local ties were among the suspects in the brutal mass murder was unsettling to local residents, who wondered whether the killers would strike again.

"It's so quiet," an employee of an Athens store complained. "It's kind of scary they don't give us any information."

The spring thaw allowed investigators to search more thoroughly for the still missing Helen Kunz. Under the scrutiny of reporters from as far away as Minneapolis and Milwaukee, they dug for three days in a manure pit but came away empty-handed.

Lone family survivor Kenneth Kunz

Finally, in late March, they found skeletal remains scattered in a marsh on a Christmas tree farm in Taylor County, about ten miles south of Rib Lake. Investigators searched the area about sixteen miles from the Kunz farm after receiving an informant's tip. They believed the remains were those of missing 70-year-old matriarch Helen Kunz.

Instead of clearing up the case, however, the discovery of Helen's remains only raised more questions, deepening the mystery. If Helen was dead, then who killed her family at the farmhouse? Why were her remains found elsewhere? What was the motive for the brutal murders?

As investigators searched the marsh for further clues, the remains and clothing were sent to the Wisconsin Crime Laboratory in Madison for forensic tests. An autopsy showed that, like her four relatives, Helen Kunz had been shot at least once in the head and murdered execution-style.

A year after the slayings, investigators still suspected Jacobs knew a lot about the murders but they continued to move cautiously. He remained charged as a party to the crime but enough evidence could not be found to upgrade the charge to murder.

"We only get one chance in court so we have to be so sure of ourselves before we go to court," Schillinger explained. Residents were concerned the killer, whoever he might be, remained on the loose. Kenneth Kunz, the lone surviving family member who discovered the bodies, had some regrets.

"Maybe, if I could have been home, they wouldn't have done it," he said. "(But) if I would have been there, I would have been gone, too."

Kenneth and other relatives wanted to tear down the house to help assuage their horrid memories. But Schillinger said the house had to remain standing, even as it grew more dilapidated and over-run with vegetation.

In late August, nearly nine months after the search of his home, Jacobs was taken into custody and charged with participating in the Kunz slayings. Besides the shell casings, tire tracks on Jacobs' car matched those found in the Kunz garden tended by Helen and Irene.

When detectives showed Jacobs a photograph of the tire tracks and told him they were B.F. Goodrich belted T/A tires, he responded that's what he had on his car. Detective Randall Hoenisch told Jacobs there weren't many tires like that around.

"Oh no, oh no, oh no, there's no way I killed somebody," he said. "Oh no. I ain't saying no more till I get a lawyer."

Kenneth Kunz also recalled that Jacobs was among four men who visited him three years earlier to look at two junk cars he had for sale. Five days after he came upon his slain family, Kunz told investigators he remembered that a guy named Jacobs bought a 1969 Oldsmobile and a 1975 Ford. The purchaser was Jacobs father but the young man had accompanied his father to the Kunz farm. The men came inside to transfer the title. Afterward, Kenneth said he noticed that a calculator, funnel and chain were missing. He called Jacobs and the items were returned the following day.

Jacobs told investigators he couldn't have committed the murders because on that Fourth of July he went to the fireworks show in Medford with a 17-year-old girl. But the girl destroyed that alibi. She told detectives she didn't even meet Jacobs until the following December.

Jacobs, of course, had been a suspect since January. Some people raised questions about why he finally was taken into custody just two weeks before Schillinger faced a primary election challenge. Jacobs had been arrested in early February on a charge of being party to the crime of murder but was released after he led investigators to the spot where he had suspiciously buried a car. Did the car contain valuable evidence?

In July, Jacobs was charged again with obstructing the investigation and two tires were confiscated from him. His mother later told authorities that after he became a suspect, her son had talked about "blowing his brains out."

Despite the multiple charges, which stopped short of actually accusing him of the crime, the case against Chris Jacobs III remained nothing more than circumstantial and, following a three-week trial in 1989, the Medford dairy farmer was found innocent of five counts of being the party to a crime of first-degree murder. Perhaps authorities hoped the legal pressure on Jacobs would cause him to confess but it never happened, possibly because he wasn't guilty.

"I was shocked," Detective Wendell Roddy, the chief investigator on the case, later said of the verdict. "I still feel there was enough evidence. I am satisfied I did my best. Maybe it wasn't good enough."

The pivotal testimony at the trial was a startling revelation by a Wausau man that he bought cocaine four times from Randy Kunz in late 1986 and early 1987. Jacobs' lawyers seized on the testimony by Tracy Bartlett, saying it was evidence that drug deals were the motive for the murders and that their client was innocent.

Bartlett, however, later was convicted of perjury after confessing that he lied about the cocaine deals.

Five years after the murders, Detective Roddy retired but said the Kunz case still haunted him.

"I don't consider it unsolved," he said. "A man was charged. He was acquitted. I have to accept that. It doesn't change the investigation. It doesn't change the evidence."

But Chris Jacobs Jr., the prime suspect's father, maintained all along that his son was framed. He blasted Roddy as an incompetent detective.

"He was an ex-grease monkey that walked out of a garage," he said. "Maybe he read Dick Tracy magazine."

The elder Jacobs said any further investigation should focus on why his son was framed and on the involvement of police officers in drug dealing.

Although he was exonerated, Chris Jacobs III said he still felt that people blamed him for the brutal murders.

"I don't trust a lot of people," he said. "I am always looking behind my back."

In July 1993, the on-again, off-again case against Chris Jacobs III was on again. A former girlfriend, Stacy Weis, came forward, claiming Jacobs confessed the murders to her in 1991. According to her story, Jacobs said he drove to Kunz house and, during an argument, he knocked Randy down and shot him. After shooting the other family members, Jacobs allegedly tied the hands of Helen Kunz behind her back, drove her to a wooded area and shot her, too.

Public Defender Weldon Nelson immediately dismissed Weis' story as the claims of "a disgruntled, jilted ex-girlfriend who threatened to get Chris Jacobs when they broke up last fall." Just before the statute of limitations ran out on kidnapping and false imprisonment, Jacobs was charged with those crimes. Once again, he wasn't charged with murder, for which there is no statute of limitations.

Did Chris Jacobs III kill five members of the Kunz family on that Fourth of July in 1987? Was it someone else after the family fortune? Were the family members executed over a drug deal gone awry? Or were the murders the result of an intra-family squabble in the bizarre household?

Chapter 18

Their calling card
Burlington, 1962

The early 1960s were a rough time for Wisconsin law enforcement officers. During an eight-month period, four officers were murdered in confrontations with suspects.

In June 1961, Waukesha Detective George Schmidling was shot to death after fatally wounding two of three burglary suspects he was taking in for questioning. In August 1961, Wisconsin Dells officer James Jantz was killed in shootout with three suspects from the Chicago area. That case is detailed in *Wisconsin Crimes of the Century*.

During the fall of the same year, Patrolman Nick Klaske of Fond du Lac was fatally wounded as he closed in on two men burglarizing a gas station.

The following Feb. 5, a Monday, Burlington Sgt. Anthony Eilers was on routine patrol shortly before 3:30 a.m. when he spotted a car dragging its tail pipe near highways W and 11. Eilers, a big man, wasn't afraid of making a traffic stop without calling for backup. At 6-foot-3 and 218 pounds, he could handle most other men.

"He's strong as an ox," said fellow officer Edward Wismefsky.

"I would have hated to tangle with him."

Eilers, 38, had served five years on the Burlington force and received his sergeant's stripes a month earlier. He had spent five years in the Army, serving in the South Pacific during World War II, where he was wounded and awarded a Purple Heart. He had worked as a roofer before becoming a cop. He was an avid hunter and fisherman who also coached a Pony League baseball team.

Although he liked the extra money and responsibility of the sergeant's job, Eilers didn't like the night hours. He didn't like being away from his wife, Dorothy, and their children, John, 10, and Jean, 8. But it never occurred to Eilers that there could be any danger in pulling over a car with a minor equipment violation. In this case, however, that confidence would be a fatal mistake.

Inside the old car were Wilson "Sonny" Brook and his brother, Max, 17. Brook, about five inches shorter than Eilers and lighter, didn't appear threatening to the strong cop. What Eilers didn't know, however, was that the two men were returning to South Milwaukee from a burglary in Janesville, where they had taken $970 from a school safe.

Sonny Brook pulled the car off the road. Eilers stopped his squad behind Brook's car. Brook rolled down his window. The sergeant flicked on his powerful silver flashlight to light his way on the dark roadway. As he approached the other car, he noticed the car's rear license plate was dangling by a single screw.

"What'd I do, officer?" Brook asked Eilers.

"That tailpipe back there," the sergeant responded. "That's a violation." Sonny Brook nervously drummed his fingers on the steering wheel. Eilers shined his flashlight over at Max Brook brother, sitting on the passenger side. He swept the light into the rear seat and it was there he spotted the cash from the Janesville burglary. "But I guess that's not all," he said. "It looks like we've got something more serious."

Brook's nervousness turned to anger as Eilers motioned with the flashlight, ordering him out of the car. He had been paroled two months earlier from prison after confessing in 1959 to burglaries of six schools. At the time of his parole, he had served two years of a five-year term. After his release, Brook had gotten a day job at the Guardian Container Corp. in Sturdevant. At night, however, he obviously hadn't given up his old habits.

As he got out of the car, Brook knew that he didn't want to go back to prison. He grabbed for the sergeant's flashlight and a life-and-death struggle began. Catching the burly officer by surprise, Brook was able to overpower him. He beat Eilers with the heavy flashlight, until the officer sunk to his knees. Then, Brook grabbed the sergeant's .38-caliber service revolver and shot him five times.

Dr. Myron Schuster would say later after the autopsy that Eilers was beaten so badly that, at first, it was difficult to tell that he also had been shot. Bullet wounds were found in his lower back, head, upper right cheek, neck, right shoulder and right side.

But Brook wasn't satisfied with the brutal murder. Now, he wanted to conceal the crime. The brothers loaded the sergeant's body into the squad and drove the two cars to a quarry, where they hoped to push the squad off a cliff into the deep water. With their own car, they rammed the quarry gate several times but failed to break it open. Brook couldn't turn off the flashing squad lights and he feared the lights and noise might alert neighbors so they left the body in the squad near the quarry gate and fled. The squad's motor was still running when Eilers' body was found several hours later. The quarry was just a block from Eilers' home, where his children slept soundly, unaware of their father's terrible fate.

When Eilers failed to make his routine check-in with headquarters at 3:30 a.m., an all-points-bulletin was issued. But the squad and the officer's body weren't found until more than two hours later, when bus driver William Boy spotted the squad with the motor running. He lived about 100 feet north of the quarry gate and was leaving for work.

But Boy had heard nothing of the scuffle two hours earlier.

"My dog didn't even bark," he said. The dog was a German shepherd that slept outside.

When officers Freddie Peklo and Richard Lichtenwalner arrived at the quarry gate, they found Eilers mangled body. His watch, rings and $4 in cash weren't taken. However, what was missing were the new sergeant's stripes from his sleeve, the flashlight, his service revolver and his hat.

When the Brook brothers got to their parents' home after the murder, they went to the basement. They hid the money and Brook washed the blood off his hands and shoes. Then, he burned his clothes and Eilers' hat. Earlier, he had thrown the gun into a snowbank along the highway near Sturdevant.

If he had been able to crash the quarry gate and get the squad into the water, Brook might have pulled off a perfect crime. The squad may not have been found for quite awhile and he might have been able to continue his night burglaries. But Brook made another mistake. He had left a calling card that led police right to him.

When the news of Eilers murder became public, Bruce Kettenberger recalled that he'd noticed the officer pull over a car early that morning on Highway 11 near Highway W.

When officers searched the area, they found the sergeant's coat in a pool of blood behind a snowbank about 15 feet off the highway. They also found a license plate.

That rear plate on Brook's car, dangling precariously by a single screw, had come off as the brothers rushed to cover up their crime. It left police the clue they needed to track down the vicious killer. In his desperate effort to turn off the squad's revolving light, Sonny Brook yanked it off the roof and stomped on it while sitting in the driver's seat. His foot hit the accelerator and the squad rear-ended his car parked a few feet ahead. The impact knocked off the plate.

Police traced the car to Brook's father, Woodrow, who lived in South Milwaukee. The elder Brook said his two sons had borrowed it on Sunday night. The car was found in a parking lot at the Bucyrus-Erie plant in South Milwaukee, where the elder Brooks worked. The car's rear plate was missing and blood was found on the seat.

After Brook was arrested, he cooperated with police. He confessed to the crime and helped them find the gun. Despite his cooperation, he received a life sentence for the brutal murder. Max Brook told police his brother "went crazy' for some reason and attacked

Eilers.

Brook's mother said a childhood injury caused her son to turn to crime.

"He fell out of a tree and hurt his back when he was little," she said. "He was about 15 when it happened. After that, his first mischievous acts started."

She said her son was in good spirits that Sunday night before venturing out with his brother to Janesville. The family hosted a party at their home.

"Sonny had been dancing and cutting up," she said. "We'd all had such a good time. I suppose I'll always remember that party."

Brook was paroled after 14 years but, by 1982, he was back in prison. Even after the long stint in prison, he couldn't give up the burglary habit. In prison, he enjoyed tinkering, sometimes building wall clocks from kits. He also studied Spanish.

In 1985, he was serving a 10-year sentence and, then in his mid-40s, he hoped for parole. He had been transferred to the minimum-security Winnebago Correctional Institution and appeared to be doing well. But Eilers' partner, Roy Knollmueller, still had vivid memories of the 1962 crime. He organized a letter-writing campaign to keep Brook behind bars. At an April parole hearing, Brook lost his temper, threatening to "get Eilers' partner" if he got out. The threat helped persuade the Parole Board to reject his request.

On Sept. 19, 1988, Brook found his own way out of prison. While running some morning errands, he drove away in a prison pickup truck and never returned. The truck was found nine days later in Madison.

After Brook's escape, the Wisconsin Department of Corrections removed all but three of the 25 lifers from minimum-security prisons and changed the inmate classification system. Corrections officials claimed the move had nothing to do with the escape and that the changes already were in the works when Brooks left.

He vanished for about a year, heading west and finding a construction job in Nevada. He might have succeeded in eluding authorities if his case hadn't been profiled several times on "America's Most Wanted." A telephone tip led authorities to North Las Vegas, where

Brook was found plastering a ceiling. He was taken into custody without a struggle. He had been working under the alias of David Giselbach.

"He tried to disguise his appearance," said Tom Nicodemus, an FBI spokesman in Las Vegas. "He dyed his hair, grew a small mustache and changed his hairstyle."

Brook's fate as a career criminal was sealed that cold winter morning on a Burlington highway. Perhaps he would have given up his burglary habit if it weren't for the murder. Or, perhaps his criminal tendencies ultimately would have led him to kill someone else.

Chapter 19

A hit man strikes

Madison, 1983

James Hudson went to work that Friday morning as usual although there was very little usual about it. The day before, Hudson had filed for divorce. It almost had been like a cloud of sadness over a failing three-year marriage enveloped the red-frame, ranch-style house for weeks. The couple's arguments had escalated to the stage of physical violence.

It was a sadness not unknown to Hudson for Carolyn was his third wife. His first wife died of leukemia and he had been divorced from his second wife. He and Carolyn had no children together but she had three children from a previous marriage to Richard Wheeler.

Despite the emotional tension or perhaps as a respite from it, James Hudson, a Madison police officer, left his home on the city's far East Side that Friday, Oct. 14, 1983, and went to work. He sat through briefing and got out in his squad. At 6:56 a.m., he was dispatched to a routine call a couple miles east of the state capitol.

After James Hudson left for work that morning, the Hudson household slowed awakened. Carolyn Hudson and children began their usual tasks — showers, toothbrush, makeup — of getting ready for the day. Mischelle, 17, Jacquelyne, 14, and Robert, 7, got ready for school.

Shortly before 7 a.m., while her husband was getting dispatched to the call on Oak Street, Carolyn Hudson heard a noise at the unlocked front door. As she walked to the door, she was confronted by a gunman she didn't know. While Mischelle looked on, the gunman fired four shots at Carolyn Hudson, then fled.

Hit man Joey Hecht

James Hudson handled his first call of the morning quickly, then received another assignment from the dispatcher. On the way to the second address, another call came over the radio that snapped his attention. It was the report of a shooting but that wasn't all. Hudson recognized the address as his own!

Joey Hecht figured he had planned this murder down to the smallest details. Hecht would be the triggerman and his sidekick, Drew Slickman, the getaway driver. Hecht didn't share many details of the crime with Slickman, who had learned not to ask too many questions of his more intelligent friend. Slickman knew Joey was up to something — perhaps a burglary — but he wasn't sure what it was.

In a rental car, they cruised through the Buckeye Road neighborhood the day before, plotting out their escape route. They watched the Hudson house, learning the family's morning routine. They had come to Madison three days before the slaying with Hecht's girlfriend, Melany Brant. The trio spent two nights at the plush Edgewater Hotel and their final night at the Exel Inn.

Sitting outside the Hudson home in the rental car with the engine running, Slickman heard the shots and watched as Hecht ran out the door, pursued by a teen-age girl, and jumped in the passenger side. At this point, he obviously realized this was something more serious than a simple burglary. But Slickman didn't question Joey about what happened. He just followed the instructions he had been given for the escape.

Despite Hecht's intricate planning, police were waiting for Slickman when he returned the rental car to the Dane County Regional Airport. Jacquelyne Hudson, who chased Hecht out of the house, had written down the license number of the getaway car.

Police put the pressure on Slickman, demanding to know the identity of his accomplice. He finally gave in, identifying Joey Hecht and adding that Hecht and Melany Brant were on their way to Milwaukee on a Badger bus. When Hecht went to pick up his luggage at the Milwaukee bus terminal, police were there to take him into custody. Melany was held as a material witness.

At first, Joey Hecht refused to admit his true identity. In San Antonio, Texas, where he had lived until shortly before the murder, he went by the alias of Bobby Brunson. He shared an apartment there with Slickman and Brant in an eight-unit building often occupied by students at nearby Trinity University. The building was sandwiched between stately, older homes of the Monte Vista historic district.

A neighbor remembered Hecht, a.k.a. Brunson, as a man big on get-rich schemes.

"He was always coming up with some big scheme to wind up a millionaire," the neighbor said. "Every time I saw him, he had another scheme lined up."

It was at his San Antonio apartment where Hecht received two envelopes addressed to "Resident." Inside were pictures of Carolyn Hudson and a typewritten note. The envelopes also contained 93 $100 bills.

"He had a wild tale about trying to meet somebody at a place where they had pre-Columbian artifacts," the neighbor said. "He told me he'd just gotten back from Guatemala, actually Belize. He talked about bringing pre-Columbian artifacts back."

Hit cases like the Carolyn Hudson murder often are difficult to solve because, when a stranger does the killing, the motive is money and difficult to track. Whoever hires the killer generally has an iron-clad alibi. This case, however, had been different. Within eight hours of the murder, Slickman and Hecht were in custody. And police investigators had a pretty good idea who hired them.

Richard Wheeler, an over-the-road trucker, was out on the West Coast when his ex-wife was murdered. But Carolyn Hudson, probably in anticipation of her break-up with James, was pressuring

Melany Brant was a key witness against her boyfriend, Joey Hecht.

Wheeler to increase the amount he paid in child support. Carolyn Hudson had seen an attorney the past summer about getting Wheeler to increase his $350-a-month payment and getting him to pay some dental bills for the children.

James Hudson recalled a conversation his wife had about four months earlier with Wheeler. After a brief conversation, Carolyn Hudson slammed down the phone.

"That son-of-a-bitch threatened to kill me!" she said.

Madison detectives John Cloutier and James Grann were assigned to the case from the beginning. Cloutier was a detective of the old school with an investigator's wisdom that comes only from working the streets. Grann, a younger detective, was nicknamed "J. Edgar," a reference to long-time FBI chief J. Edgar Hoover, for his hard work and no-nonsense approach. Within hours of the murder, the two detectives began to amass mounds of evidence they hoped would tie Wheeler to the killing.

Like pack rats, the two detectives began collecting everything they could lay their hands on that might have a bearing on the murder, even seemingly insignificant data. Grann, for example, got a complete meteorological record of the day of the murder, including time of sunrise and sunset, temperatures, sky conditions and wind velocity.

Andrew Slickman

Early in the investigation, Hudson also was viewed as a prime suspect. Five days after the murder, Grann dreaded an interview he had to conduct with his fellow officer. Less than an hour before the interview, two other Madison detectives, Mary Otterson and Keith Hackett, called from Texas, where they had been questioning acquaintances and gathering evidence on Hecht and Slickman. They also had reviewed telephone records, discovering calls from Hecht's apartment to the Wheeler's Lodi residence. It was the first link between the hitmen and their benefactor but it wasn't enough to put him behind bars.

Subpoenas were issued for bank and postal records. A San Antonio post office box was found rented to Melany Brant. Hecht bragged shortly after his arrest that he had been involved in 15 contract killings , many of them by mail order.

"A lot of it was kind of blowing smoke, although parts of it turned out to be true," Cloutier said.

Phone companies in Wisconsin, Illinois, Florida and Texas checked millions of calls against 20 names supplied by the detectives.

A district attorney special investigator, William Drenkhahn, was assigned to work with the Madison detectives on the case. They discovered a middleman helped arrange the contact between Hecht and Wheeler. He was James Stomner, owner of the La Petite Beauty Salon in Wisconsin Dells.

The case ultimately involved millions of records, at least 1,000 interviews and 2,500 pages of police reports. After 10 months, Drenkhahn and the two detectives persuaded deputy district attorney Stephen Bablitch they had enough evidence to arrest Wheeler and Stomner. The two men were arrested on Aug. 10, 1984, along with Wheeler's wife, Jaqueline, later found innocent.

Slickman pleaded innocent to a charge of first-degree murder, then made a deal with prosecutors to plead no contest to a lesser charge. He was sentenced to two years in prison. He said it came as a complete surprise that Hecht planned to murder Carolyn Hudson.

"I had no idea of his intentions or what he was involved in at all," he told the court. "When I found myself under arrest for murder, it destroyed the last vestige of self-respect I had."

Prosecutor Stephen Bablitch said Slickman probably didn't know Hecht had killed Carolyn Hudson when he turned in the rental car and allowed the clerk to stall him until police arrived. It seems unlikely that Slickman didn't have some suspicions but his cooperation with police helped persuade them to overlook that aspect of the case.

With the evidence weighted against him, Joey Hecht pleaded guilty to first-degree murder and received a sentence of life plus 53 years. The sentence included convictions for armed burglary and being a felon in possession of a firearm. It wouldn't be the last time, however, that the world would hear of him.

With Slickman and Hecht safely tucked away, prosecutors turned their full attention to Wheeler and Stomner. A three-week trial began in April 1985.

Wheeler claimed he wanted to scare his ex-wife perhaps by blowing up her car but denied he plotted to kill her. Stomner's attorney, Raymond Gross of Clearwater, Fla., rejected overtures from prosecutors that his client plead to a lesser charge. Gross believed his client was innocent.

A jury deliberated six hours before finding the two men guilty of conspiracy to commit first-degree murder. Although both received life sentences, Judge Mark Frankel indicated he believed Stomner was the lesser culprit.

Richard Wheeler   James Stromner

"It may be that he did not fully appreciate the potential criminal implications of his involvement," the judge said.

Six months after the convictions, Joey Hecht was taken from Waupun State Prison to University Hospital in Madison for treatment of a feigned illness. Outside the hospital, he produced a gun, overpowered a guard and took a man and his young son hostage. Hecht forced the man, Earl Reiner, to drive him away from the hospital but, unfortunately, Reiner's pickup truck was almost out of gas.

When Reiner stopped for gas, Hecht got out, demanded that Reiner "wait here and don't move." But Reiner grabbed his son and rushed to a cleaners to call police. Officers rushed to the scene and surrounded Hecht on the Glenway Golf Course on Madison's West Side. He fired a shot at them before surrendering.

A year later, prison guards found a .22-caliber bullet concealed in a typewriter in Hecht's cell. But Hecht used his typewriter for more than just hiding bullets. By December 1987, the contract killer had turned jailhouse lawyer, winning a state appeals court decision that allowed him greater access to law books in prison.

The appeals court overturned a decision by Dane County Circuit Judge Daniel Moeser that Hecht should abide by prison rules limiting inmates to just two law books a day.

Hecht's sudden inspiration to study the law came from a need to defend himself against the Madison escape charges which, appeals Judge Paul Gartzke said constituted a "a special need for access to legal materials."

The brutal murder of his wife took a heavy emotional toll on police officer James Hudson. He left the department and, several years later, engaged in a standoff with police when he holed up in his house with a gun, threatening to kill himself. The standoff ultimately ended peacefully but Hudson would never shake the tragic memory of his wife's violent death.

Chapter 20

Doctor of death
Milwaukee, 1991

T he bizarre story told by Tracy Edwards when he flagged down a patrol car that hot July night was difficult for the Milwaukee police officers Robert Rauth and Rolf Mueller to believe. With a pair of handcuffs dangling from his wrist, Edwards looked to them like he was drunk or on drugs. He told the officers someone was trying to kill him and that he had been "with the devil."

It probably was nothing, they thought, but they might as well check out the guy Edwards was raving about. A six-foot, sandy-haired, pale young man met them at the door of the Oxford Apartments. Despite a faint odor of beer on his breath, the man appeared sober and certainly more credible than Edwards.

Mueller headed for the bedroom to look for a knife Edwards said was used to threaten him. The officer found the knife and a Polaroid camera on the bed. He glanced up at some photographs on a dresser. At first glance, they seemed to depict men engaged in sexual acts. It was beginning to look like this whole thing was a domestic squabble between two gays. But when Mueller examined the photos more closely, he was shocked. Some of them showed the mutilation and dismemberment of bodies in excruciating detail.

That wasn't all there was to the grisly scene, however. In the freezer were packages of some kind of fleshy material. On the bottom shelf of the refrigerator in a cardboard box, the officers found a human head.

Five skulls, some painted, were removed that day from Jeffrey Dahmer's apartment as Mueller and Rauth uncovered the worst series of crimes ever committed in Wisconsin and certainly one of the most nauseating crime scenes in human history. When the body parts were identified, catalogued and added up, Jeffrey Dahmer admitted killing seventeen men and boys. But he didn't stop there. He had sex with some of the victims after death, ate some of their body parts and, in the worst living nightmare out of a horror movie, tried to lobotomize some of his victims by drilling holes in their heads and freezing parts of their brains so he could keep them alive for his own sexual pleasure.

In a literal sense, Dahmer was a doctor of death and his murders went far beyond the normal urban violence. They were crimes against humanity itself.

Through it all, Dahmer's appearance and composure belied the savagery of his acts. Far from a raging madman, he appeared to comprehend his situation. He made no claim of mind control by aliens or the devil. During hours of interrogation by police, he was calm, polite and generally cooperative. Most of the details about his crimes came from his own recollections and admissions.

Dahmer's dissections, cannibalism and necrophelia rivaled the murders and grave-robbing of Ed Gein more than three decades earlier. Unlike Gein, however, Dahmer had no readily apparent mental illness. But how could a man commit such atrocities if he were sane? The answer didn't come easily.

His interest in dissection apparently began in childhood, when he enjoyed collecting bugs and saving them in a woodshed behind the Dahmer family home in a suburb of Akron, Ohio. As he reached puberty, the hobby advanced to small animals. Occasionally a dog or cat would disappear around the neighborhood but it didn't occur often enough to raise suspicions.

Young Jeffrey was always sort of an oddball. In high school, other students would pay to watch him perform at a suburban mall. Downing a six-pack of beer in preparation for his act, he would feign seizures, scream and knock over drinks at the Woolworth's lunch counter. The performance became known as "doing a Dahmer" but he never was stopped by police or security guards.

At school, he gained a reputation as the class clown but young Jeffrey clearly was a clown with an underlying mean streak. He would do cruel imitations of people with cerebral palsy or draw chalk outlines of dead bodies in hallways.

When he graduated from high school, young Jeffrey was abandoned by his family. His father, Lionel, had moved out of the house as the marriage to the former Joyce Flint of Chippewa Falls disintegrated. Dahmer's mother and younger brother soon moved to Wisconsin, leaving him alone in the house.

About the same time, Dahmer committed his first murder. The victim was Stephen Hicks, a hitchhiker on his way to an outdoor rock concert at Chippewa Lake Park west of Akron. Hicks accompanied Jeffrey back to his home on Bath Road. When Hicks said he wanted to leave, Dahmer picked up a barbell and smashed his skull. Then he held the barbell over Hicks' throat, strangling him. Fearful of being discovered, Dahmer cut up the body, put the pieces in plastic bags and hid them under the crawl space. Later, after an unsuccessful attempt to to bury the pieces, he cleaned off the flesh and smashed each bone with a hammer, scattered the tiny fragments in a rocky area behind the house.

Dahmer didn't kill again for several years, a period he spent serving in the U.S. Army in Germany and working at a fast food restaurant in Florida. His drinking problem, however, continued unabated and his Army roommates sensed there was a secret the young man carried.

"Someday you're going to hear from me again," Dahmer predicted to his platoon leader. He was right.

After a short time in Florida, Dahmer's father, Lionel, and his new wife, Shari, persuaded Jeffrey to come back to Ohio. Soon afterward, however, the young man was in trouble again. In a final effort to help his son, Lionel Dahmer sent him to live with his grandmother, Catherine, in West Allis. Young Jeffrey always seemed fond of his grandmother and perhaps she could straighten him out.

On the surface, moving into his grandmother's suburban home seemed to have a positive effect on Dahmer. He got a job as a phlebotomist at Milwaukee Blood Plasma Inc., an ironic but perhaps not coincidental occupation in light of his later activities. But he was laid off by the following summer and soon was getting into trouble again. He was arrested Aug. 8, 1982, at the Wisconsin State Fair for exposing himself in front of a crowd. In 1986, two 12-year-old boys came upon Dahmer standing along the banks of the Kinnickinnic River. His pants were pulled down to his thighs and he was masturbating. One boy asked if he was enjoying himself.

A conviction of disorderly conduct for the incident forced Dahmer into psychological therapy but his anti-social activities would only grow far worse. By 1987, he began frequenting the Club 219, a gay bar on Second Street in Milwaukee. To other bar patrons, he seemed like a non-threatening loner but that was far from the truth. It was at Club 219 that Dahmer may have met Steve Tuomi, a white 28-year-old man who grew up in Michigan's upper penninsula. Dahmer apparently went with Tuomi to the Ambassador Hotel, where he later told authorities he woke up lying on top of Tuomi's dead body. As he had in the Hicks killing, Dahmer started to panic as he tried to devise a way to dispose of the body. He rushed to a nearby shopping mall and bought a suitcase. He stuffed the body into the suitcase and brought it to his grandmother's house, where he dismembered the corpse and disposed of the remains.

Four months later, in January 1988, Dahmer struck up a conversation with James Doxtator outside the Club 219. He offered money if the 14-year-old boy would come with him back to his grandmother's house to pose for photos. James agreed. At the West Allis house, Dahmer gave Doxtator a drink with a sleeping potion mixed into it. When James passed out, Dahmer strangled him. As he had done with Hicks, Dahmer used a sledgehammer to smash the bones into small fragments.

Less than three months later, Dahmer met Richard Guerrero, 23, in front of the Phoenix Bar, down the block from Club 219. Following what was becoming a pattern, Dahmer invited Guerrero to his grandmother's house where they could watch videos, take some nude photos or have sex. Dahmer drugged Guerrero and strangled him, then disposed of the remains.

Dahmer's activities didn't entirely escape the notice of his grandmother. During the summer of 1988, she noticed a disturbing odor in her garage and sent Dahmer's father to check it out. All Lionel Dahmer could find was a small amount of slimy, black residue he couldn't identify. That fall, however, Catherine Dahmer finally forced her grandson to move out when she came downstairs and found him with a black man. Both men were drunk. By this time, Dahmer had found another job at the Ambrosia Chocolate Co. in Milwaukee. He could afford to get his own apartment.

Dahmer rented a place and didn't waste any time taking advantage of his new freedom. The day after he moved in, he offered fifty dollars to a 13-year-old Laotian boy if he would pose for pictures. Dahmer served his customary knockout drug and began fondling the boy. But unlike the other victims, the boy didn't lose consciousness. Instead, he fled the apartment and reported the incident to police. Dahmer was arrested for second-degree sexual assault and enticing a child for immoral purposes. He was released on bail but convicted of the charges in January 1989.

Dahmer was apologetic before the judge, begging for leniency and calling the incident "the climax of my idiocy." In retrospect, Dahmer's humility was sheer duplicity and an outright lie. During the five months he awaited sentencing, Dahmer lured Anthony Sears to his apartment, served his knockout drink and killed him.

During his ten-month work-release sentence, Dahmer's stepmother, Shari, noticed a marked change in him.

"He had no light in his eyes," she said. "Jeff lost his soul in there."

But Dahmer didn't lose his penchant for killing and, upon his release, he picked up right where he left off. Raymond Lamont Smith, also known as Ricky Beeks, became the next victim. He was followed by Edward Smith, who was nicknamed the shiek because of his habit of wearing a turban-style wrap on his head. He met Ernest

Miller at a small business area on North 27th Street, lured him back
to the apartment and killed him. A few weeks later, David Thomas
became yet another victim of Jeffrey Dahmer.

During the killing spree, Dahmer met frequently with his pro-

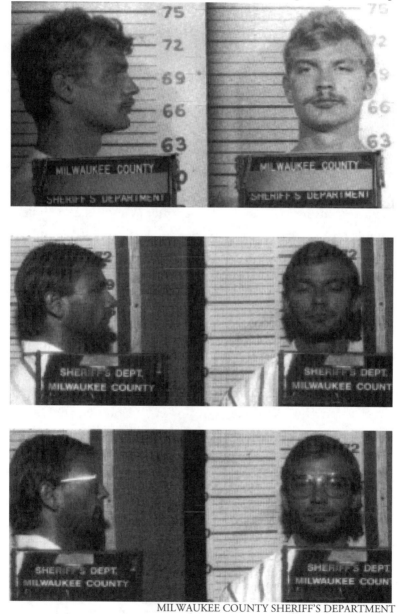

MILWAUKEE COUNTY SHERIFF'S DEPARTMENT

Jeffrey Dahmer at the time of his 1982 arrest (top) and in July
1991.

bation officer, Donna Chester. He told her he was no longer interested in boys and young males and he realized alcohol was the root of his problem. She noticed he appeared depressed, refusing to look at the positive side of anything. While appearing cooperative to Chester, Dahmer was saving the skulls and body parts of his growing list of victims back at his apartment. The following spring of 1991, Curtis Straughter, Errol Lindsay and Tony Hughes would die at the hands of Jeffrey Dahmer.

On Memorial Day weekend, Dahmer's killing spree was nearly exposed when three Milwaukee police officers visited his apartment. Body parts were hidden in various parts of the apartment and Dahmer's dissection pictures were strewn about. The officers were repelled by a pungent smell and noticed the pictures but didn't look closely enough to find out about the murders.

The incident began when Konerak Sinthasomphone, brother of the Laotian boy Dahmer had molested a couple years earlier, was lured to the killer's den. While 14-year-old Konerak was succumbing to the knockout potion, Dahmer went out to buy beer and cigarettes. Konerak woke up and ran naked into the street. Dahmer spotted the boy and tried to get Konerak back to the apartment without arousing suspicion. But two women from the neighborhood intervened and called police.

To the officers, however, Dahmer's story seemed more credible than the suspicions of the women. Dahmer lied about the boy's age and identity, persuading the officers the incident was nothing more than a spat between two gay lovers. Later, the officers would be fired for their failure to intervene and perhaps cut short Dahmer's career of horror.

After his brush with the law, Dahmer resumed killing but decided to seek some of his victims in Chicago. He met Donald Montrell of Flint, Mich. at a Chicago gay pride march and lured the young man back to his den of death. Matt Turner and Jeremiah Weinberger also succumbed to Dahmer's horror, although Weinberger survived an extra day, probably the longest relationship the serial killer ever had in his life.

By this time, Dahmer was running out of space for his growing collection of body parts. The refrigerator and freezer were crammed and parts were stuffed in dresser drawers and on closet shelves. Neighbors were starting to complain about the smell. Dahmer bought a huge vat and filled it with acid. The vat became a liquid grave for two of his unfortunate victims.

The frequency of killings increased. Dahmer became too busy managing his grisly collection to show up for work and was fired. The landlord served him with an eviction notice. That presented a real problem. How would he be able to dispose of the parts or move them to a new apartment? Oliver Lacy and Joseph Bradehoft became the final victims of Dahmer's terror.

The narrow escape of Tracy Edwards and the discovery of Dahmer's den of horrors brought a media circus to Milwaukee. Edwards sold his exclusive story to several tabloids and TV talk shows. Long before the trial, four books quickly materialized, detailing the gruesome story. Families of the victims filed multi-million dollar lawsuits to ensure that Dahmer couldn't profit from his crimes. The killer himself unraveled his incredible tales for police investigators. His only demand in return for the detailed information was that he be permitted to smoke.

For many Wisconsin residents, Dahmer's case dredged up unpleasant memories of Ed Gein three decades earlier. Gein, who killed two women and robbed graves for body parts, inspired the movies *Psycho* and *Texas Chainsaw Massacre*. But moviemakers didn't seem as interested in Dahmer's horrible story.

Actually, Dahmer's case bore more similarities to Dennis Nilsen, a London serial killer credited with fifteen murders over a four-year span beginning in 1978. Loneliness may have been an important factor for both men, who shared conflicts over their unresolved homosexual urges. Like Dahmer, Nilsen cut up the bodies of his male victims and his killing spree was uncovered when a plumber called to clean out a backed-up drain found body parts.

At Dahmer's trial in early February 1992, expert testimony centered on whether the serial killer met the requirements of Wisconsin's insanity law. In order to be judged insane, it had to be proven that he wasn't aware of the wrongfulness of his acts.

Forensic psychiatrists testifying for the prosecution and defense gave their views about whether Dahmer was insane. Focusing on the narrow standards of the law, however, the psychiatrists at the trial failed to deal with the larger question of how a man could commit such inhuman acts and lead a normal appearing life at the same time.

That answer was provided by Dr. Gary Maier, a Madison forensic psychiatrist who provided consultation for *Massacre in Milwaukee*, one of the books about the Dahmer case. Maier compared Dahmer to doctors in Nazi Germany who were able to kill in the name of healing. Both suffered from what Maier called a doubling of personalities, allowing two conflicting sets of ethics to operate simultaneously.

"I think this concept is one that makes a Dahmer more understandable," Maier said. "Because there aren't, by day when he goes to work, many clues that this is anything like a quirky guy or a guy who has unusual values. But something happens to trigger or cause this other part of himself to come out. For serial killers where there doesn't seem to be a major change in them, this process of doubling makes the most sense."

Dahmer was found sane and convicted of fifteen of the murders. At another trial two months later in Ohio, he was convicted of the Hicks killing. He is serving fifteen consecutive life terms at Columbia Correctional Institution at Portage.

The convictions didn't end the legal aspects of the Dahmer case, which moved to civil court where anyone connected with the case was suing. In April 1993, Dahmer was shackled and brought back to Milwaukee to testify in a lawsuit brought by the parents of Konerak Sinthasomphone against the Milwaukee Police Department.

Are there other Jeffrey Dahmers out there, leading normal lives by day but releasing their vicious Mr. Hyde personalities in the shadow of darkness? We can only hope not.

Bibliography

Articles published by Hancock News, Milwaukee Journal, Milwaukee Sentinel, Playboy Magazine, Rhinelander Daily News, Superior Evening News, Tomah Journal, True Detective Magazine, Wisconsin State Journal.

Balousek, Marv *Wisconsin Crimes of the Century*, Madison Newspapers Inc:1989.

Jaeger, Richard and Balousek, M. William *Massacre in Milwaukee*, Waubesa Press:1991.

Moe, Doug "Without a Trace: The Homberg Murder Case," Madison Magazine, January 1990.

Radish, Kris *Run, Bambi, Run* Birch Lane Press, New York:1992.

Rosholt, Malcolm *The Battle of Cameron Dam* self-published:1974.

Sifakis, Carl *The Encyclopedia of Crime* Facts on File, New York:1982

Twombley, Robert C. *Frank Lloyd Wright: His Life and Architecture,* John Wiley and Sons, New York:1979.

Index